BEACON LIGHTS OF GRACE

W HEN men shine as Beacon Lights of Grace it is Grace that maketh them to shine!

Gentle birth and Oxford backgrounds are not the *high enablements;* neither are meager endowments and physical inflictions the *defeating caducities.* The exploits of Heaven are always done (Daniel 11:32) by means of Charism. (Author's *Avant-Coureur*)

BEACON LIGHTS
of GRACE

By
RICHARD ELLSWORTH DAY

TWELVE BIOGRAPHICAL VIGNETTES

Amos of Tekoa
Bernard of Clairvaux
John Hambleton
Col. James Gardiner
Henry Moorhouse
George Herbert
Francis Asbury
William Carey
Christmas Evans
James Lackington
Dwight L. Moody
John Pounds

Biography Index Reprint Series

BOOKS FOR LIBRARIES PRESS
FREEPORT, NEW YORK

INTERNATIONAL STANDARD BOOK NUMBER:
0-8369-8057-3

LIBRARY OF CONGRESS CATALOG CARD NUMBER:
71-148210

PRINTED IN THE UNITED STATES OF AMERICA

To
WILLIAM B. EERDMANS

whose career
as a
Publisher of Religious Books
would make a worthy
New Chapter
for
Curwen's
HISTORY OF BOOKSELLERS

CONTENTS

CONTENTS—Continued

ILLUSTRATIONS

All drawings for this book were made by the Staff Artists of the *Religious Digest*.

The Coast Beacon serves as the illustration on the book jacket and also, as the frontispiece illustration.

The Avant-Coureur (Herald) is printed on the half-title page of AVANT-COUREUR.

The ectypes of the twelve subjects depicted in these twelve vignettes are printed, respectively, upon the chapter number pages.

AVANT · COUREUR

For Who maketh thee to differ from another, and what hast thou that thou didst not receive? (I Corinthians 4:7) The Lord doth put a difference between the Egyptians and Israel. (Exodus 11:7)

AVANT-COUREUR

THE King greatly blessed me with poor health in my youth, the outcome of which was that oftentimes, when the natural instinct would have had me tracking cottontails through bronze corn stalks and snowy fields, I went instead to the pleasant reading room of the Hoosier Library. Thus blizzards, drenching rains, and super-heated summers passed unheeded. Had I not found a Postern Gate into Romance?

There, on the shelves of that library, the King placed Certain Books, like manna in the ark, upon which my beleaguered heart did feed and was sufficed. A great conviction thereupon began to bring forth and to bud, which to this day has never declined:

Meager original endowment and physical handicaps are as light as the dust of the balance, if only the King can get the glow of His Grace upon us!

* * *

On one of those shelves down which I hungrily read was Lord's *Beacon Lights of History*.

15

Well, who ever said a boy must not dream?

So, it seemed as if a commission were tendered to write some day a series of vignettes on certain men who, right at the start, had two strikes against them; men who later found how little this meant if only He were well pleased with them.

Then, slowly it began to emerge during the library-years that, when God seeks men to shine for Him, He is not dependent upon their human excellencies. When men shine as Beacon Lights of Grace, it is Grace that maketh them to shine! Gentle birth and Oxford backgrounds are not *the high enablements;* neither are meager endowments and physical inflictions *the defeating caducities.* The exploits of Heaven are always done (Daniel 11:32) by means of Charism.

*   *   *

It has been a long time since those dreams of Wabash years. The over-thought, at first, was as an angel of encouragement: *No human frailty shall be suffered to bar men from His service.* Gradually the over-thought began to appear as an angel of purging (John 15:2): *No human excellence shall be suffered to brevet men for His service.* The light from the beacon of God is in every case a Borrowed Glow.

*   *   *

The commission is now undertaken. But it results in a far different book than if it had been written years ago. Whether God's servants are of the family of Jabez (I Chronicles 4:9) or from the School of Gamaliel (Phillippians 3:8-9) it is Grace that maketh them to differ!

RICHARD E. DAY

CEDAR-PALMS
SUNNYVALE, CALIFQRNIA

I.

A KEEPER OF NOKEDS

Amos of Tekoa

"Seek Him that maketh the seven stars and Orion, and turneth the shadow of death into the morning, and maketh the day dark with night: that calleth for the waters of the sea, and poureth them out upon the face of the earth: The Lord is his name . . ." (*Amos*) around 780 B.C. You suddenly remember that this was a half century before Romulus and Remus, suckled and saved by a wolf, founded the City of Rome. You also recall both the boys are dead, but the Wolf still lives, castled on the Tiber.

You quickly find that the city where Amos dramatically appears is Bethel, and that Bethel is the religious and political capital of Israel. Nor is it hard to see that this year 780 B.C. is the best of times. And it is the worst of times. It is the best of times for a well-fed Upper Class which panders to the fleshly appetites of men. It is the worst of times for the Underlings who can be sold into slavery for a pair of sandals. It is fine weather for the cold proud City Ladies, who walk out of their ivory palaces, satiated with costly foods, clothed in imported garments and marked by tinkling ankle-bells. It is foul weather for the submerged masses who pay for these ivory palaces and "slave-bells" with their very life blood.

It is a very ugly picture—this City of Bethel, in the year 780 B.C. Morality has all but perished; justice has surrendered to bribery, commerce to shoddy, and honest weights to false balances. Pilgrims coming into Bethel to worship are waylaid and robbed by disguised priests—the very priests to whose altars the pilgrims were bound. Fathers and sons make a night of it, and consort with the same prostitutes!

Now you begin to understand Amos a little better. He is the first of the prophets. Jonah has not yet arrived in Nineveh via the Great Fish. It is fifty years before Isaiah. And Amos, by every prudent canon, is certainly a prophet out of place. Everything about him is incorrect. He does not wear one of those new blue-wools, carded in Luz; rather he has a shapeless gray mantle over his shoulders—more like a San Quentin overcoat. And the shepherd's crook with which he thumps out his points on the cobbles of Bethel—unspeakable! Nothing seems right about Amos, preaching in Bethel! It is just as if a Zanjerro from the canals of Maricopa has suddenly appeared on Fifth Avenue with his Johnson-grass hoe!

Nothing can come out of this!

*   *   *

But something did come out of it, just the same. Amos' oratory moved the proud city like a sand storm from Tekoa. Even the king in the palace was troubled. You find that the Book of Amos gives a digest of Amos' diatribes.

His message is uniformly a five prong attack. Not *three*, like a city preacher; *five*. Four of his "heads" are nitrous indictments:

1. Social injustice
2. Demoralizing luxury
3. Moral collapse

4. Forsaking God

His mid-way peroration is that such a city, even Bethel, will soon be meat for the war dogs. Thereupon he gathers himself for his final point, and his flaming finis:

5. The Mercy of God:

> "But, saith the Lord unto the house of Israel, seek Me and ye shall live: seek the Lord and ye shall live!"

*   *   *

That fifth point is the old and constant incongruity of all Gospel preaching!

*   *   *

Just how long this "shepherd prophet" was suffered to continue his assaults against dignity is uncertain. Evidently it was some time before he was stopped. Nor do we know how he was stopped. One tradition has it that Amaziah the High Priest beat him many times; beat him to death, and Amos' broken body was buried in Luz. Another tradition says he wearily dragged himself back to Tekoa, there died and there was buried.

But Amaziah, the malicious priest, has become the symbol for portraying the eternal contest between professional religionists and naturals who have by-passed so-called higher culture. Amaziah was a well-known type. Educated in the Bethel Seminary, "his widening sympathies led him step by step to modify religion, and, recognizing the good in all, to shape the worship of Jehovah so as to conform with local ideas." He could have served splendidly as Chairman of the World Church Committee. On one point Amaziah was adamant: the prophets of religion must be academically standardized — like an army chaplain! So far as Amos was concerned, Amaziah couldn't understand it — a man from Negeb the Arid essaying to prophesy!

So he resorted to Coward's Blunderbuss—cheap sarcasm.

"Oh *you!* you *seer!* so called! You're not a prophet! neither the son of a prophet! Skip on away from here back to Judah! There prophesy. But not *here.* This is Bethel! This is the King's chapel! and this is the King's court!"

*   *   *

Amos in his reply set forth the eternal qualifications of a prophet of God:

> "I was no prophet, neither was I a prophet's son: but I was a herdman, and a gatherer of sycamore fruit: And the Lord took me as I followed the flock, and the Lord said unto me, 'Go, prophesy' . . .'"

*   *   *

Let us forego a host of truths which emerge from the ministry of Amos—such as God's doom upon decadent nations—and let us fasten attention upon one matter. Neither the message nor the messenger of God stand in need of purple and fine linen. You see that in John who, though clothed in camel's hair, yet attracted the metropolitans to a wilderness pulpit fifty miles away.

And you see it in Amos, too. His rejoinder to Amaziah needs paraphrasing. What he said was, "I am a keeper of Nokeds, and a pincher of figs." The Noked was a type of sheep you would never tolerate among your Merinos; a bench-legged, low-swung, stringy-meated animal; a sort of cactus mammal modified to stay alive in Negeb. And the figs! Low graders, like an Ontario crab-apple. Kadotas on the Tekoan Highland couldn't live out a year. Amos' figs were unable to mature their fruit. Human hands had to pinch them so as to "sour them ripe."

Such, he admitted, were the impoverished exposures of his life. But—God can find tunics in any wardrobe for His messages, and God can therein also provide culture for His servants. Therefore, it should be no occasion of surprise to find, when Amos speaks, that his language has mountain splendor. One author writes, "You'll have to go back to Dante to find anything equal to Amos' prose." We have had a bit of fancy for Dante, but we would say it this way, "Dante lighted his candles on Amos."

*　　*　　*

Sample the dignity of Amos' imagery. Having observed how lofty Cedars and robust Oaks die out on the Arabah, he remarks that it is even so with the Godless: their fruits are destroyed from above and their roots from beneath . . . He listens to the truculent squeak of an overladen harvest wagon, and says "Even so God groans under your weight." . . . He calls the mincing ladies of Bethel Boulevard "kine of Bashan," who are soon to be led away with hooks. . . . Bethel to him has the stench of the camps, but the inhabitants are nose-hardened . . . The music of their cabarets is a racket! . . . Their cultural efforts like plowing on a rock. . . .

And the lifts by which oratory and devotion alike are fired are furnished by that same simple world in which he lives. For him, the seven stars of Orion, sailing over the blue-black night sky, are altar lights in his vaulted cathedral. And when he thinks of the long-suffering Redeemer, and His Grace to usward, he makes a harvest scene illustrate the hope of an awakening. It is a classic in beauty and power:

> "Behold, the days come, saith the Lord, that the plowman shall overtake the reaper, and the treader of grapes him that soweth seed; and the mountains shall drop sweet wine, and all the hills shall melt."
> (Amos 9:13)

II.

"THE VERY THOUGHT
OF THEE"

Bernard of Clairvaux

"To me also it has been given to sit beside the feet of the Lord Jesus, and with all devotion to embrace first one, then the other . . . O Lord, I will never forget Thy justifications: they shall be my song in the house of my Pilgrimage, until mercy being exalted above judgment, then misery shall cease, and my glory shall sing to Thee forever, and not be silent." (Bernard, *The Feet of God*)

"THE VERY THOUGHT
OF THEE"

Bernard of Clairvaux

AND now, we give you Bernard! But we forbear titling him "Saint." There are those whose canonizations are not valid with us. It would be *proper* to say "Saint Bernard"; but it would also be proper in the case of *anyone* who is of the called according to His purpose. And the title, belonging to so many, does not increase the stature of either Bernard or ourselves by the using of it. It is best to let his name (or ours) shine by reason of whatever peculiar excellence it has on its own—Bernard of Clairvaux.

* * *

The previous chapter influences us to "pick Bernard up cold." Let us start towards his monastery in the hill country of northeastern France, without knowing much about him, learn what we can upon the way, and take it from there. . . . One might begin

31

the journey to Clairvaux from the city of Paris, but it is just as well to get off the odd little French train that rattles up from Cannes, at Orleans. From there, go eastward as you wish, by bicycle, bus, or tram, to the Department of Aube, and to the town of Bar-sur-Aube, thence northward ten miles to the village of Clairvaux. . . .

The calendar now shuffles swiftly backward to any year between 1114 and 1153 A.D. . . . As we leave Orleans, we find ourselves at the end of the Dark Ages. . . . We cannot properly understand Bernard when we arrive in Clairvaux unless we know something of the world in which he lived.

Readjust your outlook, for beginning right here we are in the Dark Ages. That accounts for the dismally smashed appearance of the countryside through which we are passing. What has happened? Well, for a thousand years—roughly 476 to 1453 A.D.—raw savages, like the Goths and Vandals, have been sacking the vast treasure houses of a decadent Europe: a thousand years of blood-lust and rapine. . . . As we journey along, we are forcefully reminded of the full end of any age which forgets God; a carnival of brawn and battle-lust, which finally settles down into rubble for jackals.

* * *

But how did Bernard happen to settle in this far off corner of France? We always thought of him as an Italian lad. . . . So he was: and the explanation of his coming to Clairvaux is veritable romance. Bernard was indeed a boy from Burgundy, born 1091, in the venerable old castle at Fontaines, near Dijon, where his father, Tesselin "the red-head," and his mother "Alith" ruled in feudal glory. Tesselin was "a kind of Christian Rufus," with a Caliban sense of justice, and a poorly adjusted holiness. He fought and prayed: that is, he prayed as he fought. His contrasts were fascinating; "gentle though brave; modest though strong; pious though rich." Alice, Bernard's mother, was a pale shadowy creature, a mournful mother of seven children, six sons and one daughter. Likely the noble lady lisped, which accounts for her being called "Alith." . . .

* * *

Bernard's boyhood days in the Chatillon High School were reddened by the flames of the Crusades. "Tesselin went, but never came back, and Alith talked much to Bernard about the glory of it all. . . ." As Bernard grew up, it was evident that his personal charm, keen mind, and solid worth were sufficient to launch him into any career—student, statesman, warrior, or courtier.

But how in the world did Bernard become a monk? A monk, of all things! . . . Well, three swiftly converging circumstances account for it. The first of these was a woodland canter on his charger "Burgundy," wherein while riding through bleak moors and tangled forests, he arrived at last at a chapel in the clearing. He suddenly found his heart had turned liquid within him, so he quickly dismounted, fell on his face and poured out his heart to God. This we call his conversion.

The second was the death of his beloved mother Alith, "whereby he became a man overnight." This we call his integration.

The third was the sudden access of a passion for the silvery bells of the monastery. And this we call his Heavenly Accolade. Thereafter, he swiftly became "the solitary monk that shook the world."

*   *   *

Immediately following his conversion, Bernard decided to enter the monastery, and with thirty others, whom he won by personal evangelism, began "preparatory seclusion" at Chattilon. "But why a *monastery?*" you may ask. When Bernard lived, the monastery was the one place in a hirdy-girdy world, where a decent person could escape "the battle of kites and crows."

In six months he was ready. In 1113, at the age of twenty-two, the heavy old gates of Citeaux opened to him, and "he disappeared from the world." . . . Not long after, the British monk, Stephen Harding, put a cross in Bernard's hand, gave him twelve monks, and sent the young abbot out to choose some spot in the decadent world where a new community might be founded. . . . Away they went, single file, northward through the wilderness to the headwaters of the River Aube, where it tumbles westward through through the foot hills of the Cote D'Or Mountains. "There in a deep valley, gloomy with heavy forests," he and his monks laid the foundations of the building whose name has become immortal in the Story of Faith and the History of Europe—the Abbey of Clairvaux.

*　　*　　*

Ah, there he is now, walking sandal-footed on the colored flagstones beneath the arbor. He is tall, hollow-cheeked; he wears a drab coat, poor-man's brown. When he looks at you, there is such a fire in his eyes that without his knowing it or your wishing it, you are promptly overmastered.

That was the effect he produced all of the thirty-four years he lived at Clairvaux. When he first came as a boy of twenty-four to begin the construction of these buildings, the valley was a savage, barren waste. But his spirit was so indomitable that young ladies said to their knightly lovers, "Go not near the monastery of Bernard, else he will take the sword from thy hand, and replace it with a Bible!" It is even reported that "mothers hid their sons, wives their

husbands, companions their friends" to prevent them
taking orders under Bernard. Kings were bent to
his will, and popes to his purposes! And even though
you of today may not know it, this Strange Man
of the Desolation more greatly enriches your life than
Plato or Socrates!

Why? Whence came this startling power?
Bernard himself tells us in a line:
"Jesus, the very thought of Thee!"

*   *   *

There you have it, good friends! Bernard was
so enamored of the Young Galilean that, but for his
friends, he would have starved his body in the devotion of His service. Even sleep to him was an in-
truder to be fought, which often caused him to hang
for days together on the verge of break-down.

"You don't like that? It is alien to the spirit of
modern religion? It has no semblance of today's comfortable faith?"

Quite so! And equally alien to our times is the
world-moving influence of Bernard.

*   *   *

The rare power in men like Bernard springs from
their Christo-centric passion. Spurgeon, for instance,
affirmed his love for the five points of Calvinism;
but he "loved the Jesus at the center better!" For

our part, we have no patience with any type of preaching wherein Jesus fails to be the very heartbeat—His Name, His glory, His grace, His beauty. Bernard says it this way:

"O Jesus! all the food of the soul is dry if not mingled with this Oil; is insipid if not preserved with this Salt!"

We are very grateful for men like Bernard; men to whom we may go when there is a famine in the land. We are grateful indeed to read in the records of yesterday such passages as this:

"It is Easter! let us have no more Lenten fare. Our soul is an hungered for the Pascal Lamb, for which it has been preparing itself by so long a fast!"

*   *   *

Bernard had an alarming obsession for finding Jesus everywhere. And we have noted that the more we read Bernard, the more our affection flames for Jesus. Before he died he wrote eighty-three homilies on the Song of Solomon, and got no further than the third chapter!

*   *   *

One of the great gifts Bernard left posterity was his poetry. What words could more earnestly express a Christian's gratitude for the passion of Jesus than these:

> "O sacred Head, now wounded;
> With grief and shame weighed down,
> How scornfully surrounded,
> With thorns Thine only crown:
> O sacred Head, what glory,
> What bliss, till now, was Thine,
> Yet, though despised and gory,
> *I joy to call Thee mine!*"

When we read or sing Bernard's songs, all the burnt hills of Moab break forth into springs and fountains! He makes us feel we'll have no religious songs from which Jesus is missing.

Here is another of Bernard's songs; we've wanted to quote it from the beginning:

> "Jesus! the very thought of Thee
> With Sweetness fills my breast,
> But sweeter far Thy Face to see,
> And in Thy presence rest!
>
> No voice can sing, no heart can frame,
> Nor can the mem'ry find,
> A sweeter sound than Jesus' Name,
> Thou Saviour of mankind."

The sentiments of Bernard's verses were not ecstatic interludes to be laid aside in ordinary hours. His ruling passion in everything he did was—Jesus!

*   *   *

Some day, if the lamps at Cedar Palms burn long enough, another volume of devotions is to appear.

Already the pages are coming into place. It shall bear the title, *A Bundle of Myrrh*:

> "A bundle of myrrh is my Well-beloved unto me!" (*Canticles* 1:13).

And had it ever been a fashion to dedicate books to saints in glory, this book would be dedicated to my beloved Bernard. He it was who first taught my eyes to see in this text the Light of the World!

III.

THE PASSING OF A HARLEQUIN

John Hambleton

"Now the Devil was loath to give me up. For years past he had me as a drudge, amidst all the fictions of a theatrical career, filling my mind with vanities; and, my constitution being broken, he had all the more access to my vain imagination to work his wiles on body and soul . . . The Devil was in earnest to keep me because he is aware that those who have been his greatest slaves are often, when converted, used for Christ with greater danger to the Devil's Kingdom of Darkness." (*From Hambleton's Sermons*)

THE PASSING OF A
HARLEQUIN

John Hambleton

THE decade 1854-1864 witnessed the appearance of a group of *gaucherie* revival bellwethers in England and Ireland—a precious flock of black swans, who hopped at a bound from their lowly beginnings to the Tower of the Flock. One of these preachers, for instance, had been a pigeon-flyer; one a fiddler from the Dog and Duck. One was a coalpitter; another a dogfighter, to whom the headline, "man bites dog," had no news value whatever. Several were prize-fighters (non Marquis of Queensbury), "Hallelujah Pugilists!" There was a chimney sweep, "a Newry Blacksmith." . . . Naturally, this was very shocking to contemporary gentlemen of the cloth—professionals who were confirmed in the idea that a dominie just had to have *a standard seminary* behind him. It was annoying no end that the labors of such bumpkins should be accompanied by another awakening.

We have no explanation for the above, save to affirm it is a mystery: the mystery of the Beacon Lights of Grace. The Book sheds a bit of light upon the whole question, wherein it speaketh of God's strange choices:

> "But God hath chosen the foolish things of the world to confound the wise; and God hath chosen the weak things of the world to confound the things which are mighty; and the base things of the world, and the things which are despised, hath God chosen, yea, and the things which are not, to bring to nought the things that are: that no flesh should glory in His presence." (I Corinthians 1:27-29)

*   *   *

A biographer cannot afford to show any patience towards *arcana imperii*. (And that, good reader, means "state secrets." Pardon, for breaking the Loom Thread.) A biographer must deal with the whole truth about his Sitter (even if it makes the Sitter look like Dorian Gray). Therefore, it must be recorded that the flaming evangelist John Hambleton began his life as a "ham" actor, a British vaudevillist from the Play House of Bad Taste.

Among his props were plumpers which enabled him instantly to look like Henry VIII, with his arctoid jowls, doing a delectable love scene with a court-lady. He possessed an assortment of fearful wads, transforming him at will into a hunch-back; or, placed beneath his vest, into a dietetic cripple. Alas, those were grisly days in the theatre, when one of the chief monkeys in the trick bag was to produce a dwarf or a monstrous cripple. (Let us go no further with this, or we might find ourselves right in the Saratoga Trunk.)

Hambleton had shoes so outrageously long that their board-slapping was always good for a deep, abdominal laugh. . . . The way he plied the slap-sticks midships on his fellow-actors always rolled his audiences in the aisles. . . . In his dressing room he had a gorgeous sofa, purchased with his own funds—purchased because of its elegant legs. Thereon he could loll like a prince—like a Great Profile. He had, moreover, a line of turbulent sex-patter, so intimate that it would embarrass an Embarcadero stevedore. Hollywood talent scouts who may read of John Hambleton will deeply regret that he did not live in 1947.

And now the truth is out; and it is better to have it that way. To his later—his Revised—tastes, Hambleton seemed to himself "like a slimy thing, crawling out of a sewer."

*　　*　　*

Yesterday's records are none too legible, but it would appear, by a little calculation, that Hambleton was born, 1819, in the city of Liverpool. Now, Liverpool even in "its modernized form" (Liverpool Chamber of Commerce) has always seemed a very formidable city; a sombre front gate for the even more sombre Irish Sea. . . . You look at the top of a down-town building, and view a giant Liver (long "i") with its wide stone wings arched above the gloomy streets. The Liver was originally intended to represent the Eagle of St. John, but the Liverpool climate could likely have been responsible for making it the fowl black-sheep it is. At any rate, the Liver gave the town its name. One is pleased to leave Liverpool (short "i") and return to London—or even to Dublin.

Liverpool began as a fishing town behind a mud wall, which Prince Rupert playfully knocked over in 1644. By the time Hambleton was born, it had become a City Dreadful, a regular Dickens' Hodge Podge. . . . Young Hambleton ran away to sea at the age of fifteen, and for seventeen years roamed the world in smelly little wind-jammers. He had long, tapering fingers, "a slender head, somewhat horsey," a magnificent voice—the precise specifications for an actor. It is no surprise to find him, presently, barnstorming the port cities of the world.

In 1850, he was billed in San Francisco's Barbary Coast. But to the theatre world of San Francisco he was intolerable. They hated him: "his nasty sarcasm;" his easy success; the way he stormed his audiences. He barely survived a number of plots against his life.

Somewhere in San Francisco's underworld, he entered the ancient mystery of Conviction of Sin. So mightily did the Spirit assault him that he decided to return to Liverpool to visit his family. They might help. They were humble Christians. He was not sure any of them still lived; was it not seventeen years since he put to sea, a wayward boy? He sailed from the Embarcadero in the storms of mid-February, 1851, and six weeks later, April 1—six weeks of interminable storms— he landed in Liverpool. He tells us that, so soon as the ship scraped the dock, he prayed:

"O God, as a fool I have climbed the ladder of folly all my days! Now, Lord God, do Thou give me understanding! Make me from this time wise to know Thee, that my soul from this hour may climb *the ladder Jacob saw*, whose top reached to Heaven!"

*   *   *

He made his way along "the wet docks" of the Mersey Estuary, shouldering his leathern sea trunk; along the shabby streets to a little cottage. "Did they still live, *any* of them?" Alas, they were all in glory save "two elderly sisters, even then in the furnace of affliction, but none the less, more than conquerors." Miserably, in the little cottage, Hambleton groped for the Gates of Life. . . .

First, he took from his sea-trunk all his vaudeville properties: his theatrical books and Babylonish garments. These he burned. . . . And the sisters watched in silence. . . . But "this work of the flesh left him still without peace. . . ." And the sisters watched in prayerful silence.

Fearing he had committed the unpardonable sin, "with remorse for the sins and follies of the past he turned to suicide." And the sisters kept a tearful vigilance before the Throne of Grace. . . . One night he locked himself in his little room, spent the night in prayer and Bible reading. And the sisters kept to their knees at their bedside.

Somewhere in that long night, before dawn, the Angels of God rejoiced over a sinner who had gotten into the Mercy House. "Joy took the place of agony: he tasted the sweets of liberty: was graciously delivered from his fears, and Jesus filled his heart with peace." Even Liverpool, in the wet dawn, looked beautiful! And the sisters wept with joy.

On the morrow he was "led to Mr. Lowe's little chapel on the East Bank." Mr. Lowe took his text from Colossians 3:3-4:

> "For ye are dead, and your life is hid with Christ in God. When Christ, *who is our life* shall appear, then shall ye also appear with Him in glory."

As the preacher portrayed a soul quickened by God's Spirit, Hambleton's joy was great, "he knew he had already passed through death unto sin, and into a new life unto righteousness."

*   *   *

Immediately following his conversion, his nights were challenged by dreams, which greatly exercised him to wonder if the Lord intended him for preaching the Gospel. In one dream a man appeared, crying bills about the town, saying in a loud voice, "You will find it written in the first chapter of the prophet Jeremiah, and the fifth verse." He awoke and looked up the text:

> "Before I formed thee in the belly, I knew thee; and before thou camest forth out of the womb I sanctified thee, and ordained thee a prophet . . ."

"His knees trembled violently. He carried the Bible to the room of his sisters. They seemed not at all surprised. They were silent. But both kissed him." You see, the sisters had been having some earnest sessions with the King, along just that line.

*   *   *

Herewith began a new chapter in the Romance of Preaching. We confess deep regret that the book-length record of John Hambleton's ministry must be left to someone else; this vignette has not the space. But—whosoever you may be who feel called to write

—dream your pages out in Liverpool! Give all the time and pains required, and you will bless the world with a book which the angels will joyfully read as you write!

Your book will tell with fuller detail how he began to preach. One day, shortly after his conversion, Hambleton attended the Yorkshire Fair "to testify as he could for Christ." The drunkenness and cursing made him heartsick. There was a spur-wall, ten feet high, one end of which was against a building, and immediately above the wall, a window opening into a public house. Therein drunkards were in a rowdy mood, singing lewd songs to Gospel music.

"The Lord seemed to say to me, 'Mount the wall!' So I mounted the wall and stood silent as a statue, without hat, and an open Bible, for an hour and a half." The effect was tremendous. The rowdies came out of the saloon, a great crowd gathered, gazing up at the silent figure. Thereupon street preachers began to address the mob with fiery effects. Hambleton always laughed about himself, as "the Fool on the Wall! Decent folks wouldn't do a thing like that. Likely the Lord never asks them to." But for his part, he'd be glad any time to act as a fool for Christ.

Your book also will tell to worth while length about his pulpit strategy. Hambleton had learned in the theatre how to "vamp his part," which made him master of open air preaching. One day, while he was speaking upon total depravity, a spiritualist cried out, "You're wrong! Man is not depraved! A child coming into the world is like a clean sheet of paper." Hambleton immediately turned to his heckler: "Bring your paper here friend, and let us examine it." The spiritualist came forward eagerly. Hambleton pointed at the man and asked, "Then why do children die if the sheet is clean? Because they are born in sin! Defiled in birth! Otherwise they would be clean and free from corruption. . . ." An Irishman shouted at the retreating spiritualist, "Och! your sheet of paper is clane dirty!"

*   *   *

That book will yield valued suggestions for modern gospel generalship, of which this one example is cited. Hambleton hired a large hall in Liverpool for an all day's preaching service. "A week of prayer was first held, that the Spirit of God would descend in power. It would certainly appear that God honored the week of prayer. On the early morning of the day's service, a company of Christians gathered spontaneously at James' Lamp, and began to march toward the hall, several blocks away, singing:

> "The blast of the trumpet so loud and shrill,
> Will shortly re-echo o'er ocean and hill!
> When the mighty, mighty, mighty trumpet sounds!
>   Come away! Come away!
> O, may we be ready to hail that glad day."

The effect of this spontaneous strategy was to bring hundreds from all directions. Reginald Radcliffe and Hambleton were so impressed by the possibilities of this plan that they formed companies of half a dozen singers each, and dispatched them to many points over Liverpool. Then the bands again converged toward the hall, singing the same song. They "were followed by poor harlots and drunkards, broken by the mighty power of God: the hall was filled, and Lime Street packed. Preachers in the street began spontaneously to address people within hearing of their voices. All day long until midnite souls were crying out for mercy, rich and poor alike; ladies in silk and poor ragged girls, gentlemen and thieves, down on their knees together imploring pardon. In the hall, meanwhile, Hambleton preached with great power. . . ."

＊   ＊   ＊

His theatrical graces, so carefully groomed for the devil, now became subdued and sanctified. And those long, elegant fingers, once flexed for the power of Hell, became obedient to Amazing Grace, beckoning great companies of sinners into the Mercy House.

He became associated with that galaxy of revival giants which suddenly appeared like constellations in British and Irish skies; men like Reginald Radcliffe, Edward Usher, Richard Weaver, Joshua Poole, Tom

Castle—and *Henry Moorhouse!* (Hambleton became young Moorhouse's teacher, of whom we will speak more in another chapter.) These "Hot Hearts for Christ," largely recruited from the Ragged Fringe, assaulted Shaw's Brow, James' Lamp, Hyde Market, The Blue Pig, the White Pig and the Boar's Head in the Name of their Lord; and, as General Booth would have started it, "Sinners marched home to glory!"

*   *   *

How does it happen that men like Hambleton become Beacon Lights of Grace? Well, you see, men of this kind are Heaven's favorite material. Thoroughly beaten, altogether defeated, such men acknowledge no excellence *in themselves!* No merit save in *Him,* and by *Him,* and for *Him!* Thereupon God irradiates them with the Charisms of Glory.

IV.

A GENTLEMAN OF THE SWORD

Colonel James Gardiner

"Oh, if I had an angel's voice,
And could be heard from Pole to Pole;
I would to all the listening world
Proclaim Thy Goodness to my soul."

(One of Col. James Gardner's favorite verses)

A GENTLEMAN OF THE SWORD

Colonel James Gardiner

N<small>O</small> AGREEMENT can be reached upon the *raison d'etre* of biographical literature, for there are at least half a dozen persuasions. One group esteems the Horatio Alger approach as having the highest value: poor boy marries banker's daughter, etc. The Pulitzer School of Journalism has no awards for any biographical works which do not "teach patriotic and unselfish service to the people." Another school desires that biography should demonstrate Faith's ability to mature its fruit in any climate: "Saints in Caesar's household." . . . Perhaps the highest motive for writing Life Stories, however, is "to spread a warm and lively sense of religion."

Now, if it be desired to find a subject attractive to all groups, we suggest the person of Colonel James Gardiner, "A Gentleman of the Sword." Whatever one likes best in biography—success story, patriotic ideals, moral victory, or the glory of faith—the career of Colonel Gardiner just has everything!

*   *   *

There is a tiny verbal cameo of Colonel Gardiner which we immediately lay upon this page as a means of better understanding him. Our hero is in the heyday of his life, exuding success, a mature British officer, clothed in a colorful dragoon uniform, riding horseback through the forests, and followed at a respectful distance by an attendant on horseback. All of this may be seen in the cameo, including his resplendent gift sword. And by reason of literature's four dimensional powers, you know what is going on in the gentleman's mind; he is praying:

"How joyous the moments when time permits me to give glory and honor and praise unto Him that sitteth on the throne, and to the Lamb forever and ever! My praise begins from a view of Thee whom I saw pierced for my transgressions. Here in this forest I summon the hierarchy of Heaven to join with me! Yea, I am certain the very larks in the fields vie in my emulations!"

Literature's four dimensional powers also enable us to see what manner of man Colonel Gardiner was, even as he rides away horseback. His waist is waspish, his shoulders meatily square, a boon which comes from hours with the foil. Though he is fifty, and though fatigues and dangers are recorded on his countenance, he is "remarkably graceful and amiable(!)" He is over six feet, strongly built. Eyes smallish, dark gray; forehead "pretty high"; "nose of a length and height no way remarkable, but well suited to the rest of his face; cheeks not very prominent." Mouth, pleasantly full. Chin a bit peaked. Voice strong with lively accent. Address, perfectly easy and obliging, the product of candor and benevolence, improved by the deep humility of divine grace and the benefit of the company of persons of distinguished ranks and polite behavior.

*   *   *

Now that's a very trig picture, good reader, and a far comelier figure than you will ever see riding through the title shots of the cinema world. But the sad part about the matter is that our Good Rider has all but vanished from the world's memory, and this particular vignette is the only place where he rides again. Even in his own time, there was but one account written of our Gentleman of the Sword, this brilliant soldier and fiery evangel; and the writer of that account was Philip Doddridge.

Do you inquire, "Not, surely, the Doddridge who wrote, 'O Happy Day that fixed my choice' "? That is correct! The very Doddridge who nearly two centuries ago gave the Church at least twenty hymn book immortals; the very Doddridge who gave Faith such stirring rubrics as,

"The hand that bears creation up
Shall guard His children well!"

Doddridge had a warm heart, but a somewhat tedious pen when it came to prose. If you doze easily, his *Life of James Gardiner* will not interfere. However, the parson's biography of the soldier, if one reads resolutely, conveys a warm sense, indeed, of religion.

You find that our brilliant officer was personally at the head of his troops in every field of valor; and at last, in the battle of Prestonpans, stayed and died almost alone, when his troops fled in disorder before the Jacobites. But you also find that fighting was casual with him: "He used constantly to rise at four in the morning, and to spend his time till six in the secret exercise of devotions, in which he contracted such a fervency of spirit as I believe few men obtained. . . . In all his warfare he endured as seeing Him Who is invisible. . . . If at any time the troops moved before six, he arose proportionately early— two o'clock!"

Whether in active campaigns, or at home on furlough, our valiant soldier cherished the things of God. "As a certain Communion Sunday approached he was quartered with his troops in the Hills of Patrick. . . . He took a walk upon the mountains that are over against Ireland. 'Ah (he exclaimed as he walked),

I shall be happy tomorrow, my soul being fed with the Bread of Life which came down from heaven!' " Later, when he wrote "his daily letter to his Lady and his children," he said: "After I had wrestled with the Angel of the Covenant, how blessed the solemn ordinance of the Lord's Supper appeared to me!"

These hours of devotion opened his understanding of certain invaluable military secrets. Thereby he realized "how mean a man can look in the transports of passion. So I resolved never to use any such freedom with my soldiers as to fall into such transports before them. Men in the lowest ranks of life know how unfit officers are, to govern others, who cannot govern themselves."

He was disgusted with any kind of military government which was thoughtless of the troops or horses. "It was brutalizing to permit the duties of the parade to interfere with the duties of the Sanctuary . . . soldiers must not be employed with their arms or their horses at seasons of public worship. . . . Faith is the surest method of attaining all desirable success in military interests."

His Hours Alone also solved the touchy problem "of being a tender and condescending friend toward his soldiers; yet, withal, keeping inferiors at their distance, thus escaping the familiarities which degrade the superior." . . . Someone in his latter life challenged him to a duel; this he declined with a calm and truly great reply: "The sword scar on my cheek came when as a boy I had a duel with a boy much older than myself. Three other duels I fought before I attained the stature of a man. But *now*— I fear sinning, and you know I do not fear fighting."

*   *   *

Colonel Gardiner was born January 11, 1688, and grew up in that tense atmosphere of English history when Stuart pretenders warred for the crown. At the age of fourteen he became a British soldier in Dutch service; at nineteen he was wounded in the battle of Ramilies; by the age of twenty-six he was a high military officer.

But his early life was distributed between a series of hot military actions and a hectic series of criminal amours, a battery of vicious indulgences. . . . In July 1719, his thirty-second year, he spent an evening with a gay company, in the midst of which he "made an unhappy assignation with a married woman whom he was to attend exactly at twelve." But the tryst was never to be kept.

He went to his room to kill a tedious hour, picked up Thomas Watson's *Heaven Taken by Storm*, started to read; likely dozed away, when suddenly, dreaming or waking, an unusual blaze of light fell upon the book. . . . He lifted up his eyes, saw Christ on the cross, heard a voice say, "O sinner, did I not suffer *this* for thee! and *these* are *My* returns!"

He was fully awake now. His heart stood still. The date at twelve seemed unutterably sordid, and "so dissolved he did not again recall the detestable assignation. He walked his apartment all night in a tumult of grief; he appeared to himself the vilest monster in the creation of God. How scandalously the devil had befooled him all these years!"

Weeks went by with Colonel Gardiner under old-time conviction. One night in October, Romans 3:25-26 flamed down from heaven, as it were, and glowed in his heart:

> "Whom God hath set forth to be a propitiation through faith in His blood, to declare His righteousness for the remission of sins that are past, through the forbearance of God; to declare, I say, at this time His righteousness: that He might be just, and the justifier of him which believeth in Jesus."

Up to that very moment he felt God's justice *required* the damnation of a sinner like himself. Then of a sudden, he saw that divine justice was not only *vindicated* but *glorified in* saving him by the blood of Jesus.

*   *   *

Thereupon followed "the first joys of salvation," which in Colonel Gardiner's case extended seven years; followed in turn by the steady glow of his walk with Jesus for more than a quarter of a century.

We look with admiration upon the unfolding of Colonel Gardiner's life story; look until a wild Highlander, armed with a scythe on a pole, pulled him down from his horse near the salt pans of Preston, September 21, 1745. "He got a deep wound, on his right arm, and his sword dropped from his hand."

*   *   *

We watch our Gentleman of the Sword ride off this page and out of memory. But some day in glory we expect to say, "Good friend Gardiner, thou didst give us Divine Heartburn to find thee so devout, and to see thee faithful unto death!" And we are certain he will reply:

> "Great is thy work," my neighbors cried,
>   And owned the power divine!
> "Great is *Thy* work," my heart replies,
> *"And be the glory Thine!"*

V.

AUCTION BLOCK SEMINARY

Henry Moorhouse

Now that I've finished as a pastor, I've found exactly the kind of preaching that brings and sustains revivals, the kind that will energize a minister after romance has hardened into duty. It is the sort which begins by majoring on the theme, "This shall my song in eternity be, O what a wonder that Jesus loves me!"; and continues the same theme through a pulpit lifetime. That kind of preaching is continuously overwhelming. Here in Cedar Palms for the first time solemn regrets are present. I wish I could live it all over again. (*Sketch Book*)

AUCTION BLOCK SEMINARY

Henry Moorhouse

IF ONE were compiling a list of border-line occupations, such as the butler, the garbage man, or the pig-sticker, then the Auctioneer would certainly have a prominent place. The Auctioneer is not a late comer to civilization, like the Fission Investigator. You may track him back across the centuries, blathering away to the amusement of his auditors, and signifying his "Sold to the gen-tle-man!" with the smart crack of his hammer on the auction block.

If any one imagines the auctioneer is lacking in color, not to be compared with a blacksmith, we hope such an one will find Pope's unforgettable lines about the auctioneer; or, Dryden's

> "That man with
> Auctionary hammer in his hand."

The auctioneer has an abundance of color. He is as ingenious as a medicine doctor, with such devices as the auctioneer's stubby candle: the sale must

be made before it burns out. Plenty of color indeed!
His 1947 successor has a place on the national hook-
up, plugging for a borderline business with his amazing *flux de bouche.*

And that reminds us: the auctioneer's tongue is
his chief instrument, turning verbal corners with
fascinating felicity. . . . But one does well to watch
carefully as he listens to the auctioneer, or he is apt
to find himself neatly flimflammed. English juris-
prudence was as hard put, in legally controlling the
auctioneer, as United States courts are with the
"bucket shopper."

Well—the foregoing etcher's lines are to let you
know Henry Moorhouse was an auctioneer. He was
born, 1840, in Lancastershire, in the shadows of the
cathedral. His boyhood days were a super-pattern
for the Dead End Kids. He was a detention home
candidate before his teens. Since he had a glib tongue,
it seems perfectly natural to find him in his later
teens behind the shaky high table, one board atop
a slim post, which he called his "block." So we go
down to the butter and egg area of Manchester, on
a certain day in 1859, to look our hero over. He
is as dimunitive as an Epsom jockey and, by reason
of a diseased heart, becomingly trim to the end of
his days. His face is deeply seamed with sin-lines,
but somehow his blue eyes move you to trust him,
though you know he is a crook. And that voice!

How it eases its way into your liking by its flashing mellowness and grace!

However, on this certain day in 1859, Henry Moorehouse is at the end of his own candle, and the Devil is about "to knock him down." Even as he rattles along, his mind subconsciously decides to escape the Cul-de-sac, into which he has come, through the suicide door. . . . That night we find him under a flickering gas jet in the hall of a cheap Manchester rooming house, with a pistol at his temple and a finger on the trigger. But—right then the voice of a man came down from a room above! A man reading:

> "How many hired servants of my Father have bread enough and to spare, while I perish with hunger. . . . I will arise and go . . . and say to my Father, Father I have sinned against heaven. . . . "

The pistol dropped from his hand, and for the next three days and nights Moorhouse wandered the streets of Manchester under old time conviction. Late the third night, he stumbled down the basement stairs of a Manchester warehouse, found an old fireman who knew just what to do. The fireman began the work of putting Henry's feet on that great Rock Foundation with Romans 10:9, 10:

> "That if thou shalt confess with thy mouth the Lord Jesus and shalt believe in thine heart that God hath raised Him from the dead, thou shalt be saved. For with the heart man believeth unto righteousness; and with the mouth confession is made unto salvation."

When Henry came up the stairs, there was the soft glow of stars in his eyes. . . . A few days later he stood listening to Richard Weaver preaching. Once in his sermon, Weaver lifted his face and shouted, "Jesus!"

That did it! Young Moorhouse knew immediately he was a new creature in Christ. "Zacchaeus went up the sycamore tree a sinner: and he shinnied down a saint. And he (Moorhouse) had stumbled down a stair hell-bent, and had come up again with Jesus at his side!" That word "Jesus" became the sweetest word he knew.

*   *   *

Almost immediately, Henry decided to become a preacher. Of all things! Why is it that almost every bounder thinks of this when he gets saved? Good reader, he just can't help it. Into his new heart comes a Voice saying,

> "Go to thy house, and unto thy friends and tell them what great things the Lord has done for *thee!*"

Yes, he would become a preacher. "But no one was interested enough in the little runt to suggest a seminary, so, fortunately, he escaped that." Not knowing what else to do, he continued at the auction block, "using every moment of his spare time just reading the Bible." In four years, he was Bible-saturated, and so continued until he died twenty years later.

*   *   *

One day an old eccentric, whose name no one took pains to record, blasted him out of the block forever. This unknown wore a long beard, was hatless, had about his shoulders a shawl of green baize, wore boots and leather breeches. He stood listening for a moment to Henry's singing out his figures. Then with terrible emphasis he shouted, "Thou ought to have thy Bible in thy hand, and out among the people, and not that hammer of the Devil!"

*   *   *

We might consider this old eccentric as graduating Moorhouse from his Auction Block Seminary. Moorhouse often said, "That short, terrible speech fell like a thunder-bolt on me. I dropped the hammer, hurried to Liverpool, and sought out John Hambleton." (See Chapter III, *Beacon Lights of Grace*). The converted actor was immediately attracted to Moorhouse, and took the youngster under his tutelage. "The lonely man felt rich in the affection and enthusiasm of the boy." Hambleton became his teacher "at the side of a haystack, or in a private room, or in a corner in a railway carriage—wherever the man and boy could find a quiet spot for Bible study."

In three years the work was done, and Moorhouse was ready for world conquest. The letters of Hambleton to his successful young protege are a part of the literature of rejoicing. He wrote Henry continuously when Moorhouse was on his four trips to the United States.

He rejoiced in the great crowds that attended Moorhouse's ministry; was peculiarly pleased when Princeton was moved like the tides of the sea under Henry's series of "addresses." Many a Princeton dominie of the last generation has said, "It was Moorhouse who set my heart on fire when I was a student." And when Moorhouse, still a youngster less than forty, died December 27, 1880, the old actor Hambleton helped bear his coffin to the Ardwick Cemetery in Manchester. After the crowd had filed out of the graveyard, Hambleton fell to his knees in a prayer that was not in any sense theatrical.

Moorhouse's peculiar ministry lay in his emphasis on *the Bible itself.* He always carried a big limp copy in his hand as he preached. In America he gave "Bible readings" in the parlors of rich and poor alike. He really didn't need his Bible as he quoted scores of relevant texts in that smooth auction block delivery; "but it did look good to see Henry standing there, like a little angel, with the Book in his hand, and the

Word on his tongue." Scores of men declared: "He made the Bible a new Book to me."

*   *   *

If you summarized the ministry of Moorhouse, you could say he has exerted a tremendous influence on contemporary faith. The great Moody Bible Institute itself stands on a stream at whose headwaters was the influence of the Little Auctioneer. And we can tell you just how it came to pass.

When D. L. Moody was in Dublin on his first British visit, Moorhouse went over to hear him, and saw Moody was "Bible deficient.", At the close of the service he said to Moody, "God will make a great preacher of you if you will preach His word instead of *your* word." Moody made up his mind then and there to dislike Moorhouse. The first time he heard Moorhouse preach—in Moody's own pulpit in Chicago! — he said, "I just couldn't keep the tears back. Moorhouse made me see just how much *God* loved *me!* And I saw Bible preaching was the only sort worth while." That, next to the power of God, accounts for D. L. Moody more than any other factor; and in consequence, Moody Bible Institute.

*   *   *

Of the Moorhouse cottage and his home life at 55 Tiverton Street, Manchester, but little may be said. That humble little house became a shrine where

Christian great hearts went to rejoice in Moorhouse's love for his "Mary," and his little daughter, "Cripple Minnie." For Minnie's sake Moorhouse often made long trips across the sordid city to minister to children in poverty. Once he took a "three penny doll" to a little girl who lay a-dying. He said afterward, "The little thing looked at it; then she put her hand into the bed, and took out some old rags. She said, 'I have been trying to make a doll myself, but I have got a real one now.' Then she kissed it. How glad that made me! And the next day the happiness I had in seeing my own little Minnie was ten times more, because I knew another little girl was made happy too!"

* * *

In some respects, however, Henry never did leave the Auction Block. He had an almost childish delight in visiting American toy stores. Once he saw a big mechanical rodent—he called it in his Lancashire dialect, "a Wat"—and explained, "My, I would like to auction that thing off in my country!" Immediately he added, "However, I've got better business now." . . . When his failing heart made it impossible to address great crowds any longer, he "put his auction block on wheels," in the shape of three "gospel carriages." The hearts of Christians chuckled with glee at the sight of him on the rear of these carriages, selling thousands of Bibles at reduced rates—Dutch

Auction in his best old time Auctioneer Patter. The British *Word and Work* was deeply amused at one occasion when "in less than an hour, he sold five hundred copies of the Bible, *chiefly to those who already possessed one!*" In 1879, his three Bible carriages sold 50,000 Bibles and Testaments: in 1880, 70,000 copies, at a total operating expenditure of $1,500.00. This fact brought Dr. George C. Needham, one time pastor of Moody Memorial Church, Chicago, to the boiling point: "What a rebuke is the work of this unassuming and sick brother in his closing days to 'societies,' 'committees,' and 'organizations'! And what a rebuke to us all who *play* at saving souls!"

*   *   *

There was victory in the little Manchester cottage on Tiverton Street December 27, 1880. Though in great anguish, Henry talked continuously of "Precious Jesus," and his last words were addressed to "Little Cripple Minnie," kneeling beside the bed: "Remember, my dear girl, God *is* love!"

VI.

SAINT'S ⸱ BELL

George Herbert

"The shepherds sing; and shall I silent be?
  My God, no hymne for Thee?
My soul's a shepherd, too; a flock it feeds
  Of thoughts and words and deeds;
The pasture is Thy Word: the streams, Thy Grace
  Enriching all the place.
Shepard and flock shall sing, and all my powers
  Out-sing the daylight houres."
                    (*The Temple, page* 102)

SAINT'S · BELL

George Herbert

HAD you walked the roads of the village of Bemerton during the years 1630-1633, you would have witnessed a noteworthy circumstance. Twice every day, 10 A. M. and 4 P. M., when the bell of the Anglican Church sounded out from the little brown steeple, "the meaner sort of the parish would rest their plows in the furrows, and after a time return to them." Let us cross the field to inquire just what this meant.

"Why sir, that was Mr. Herbert's Saint's-Bell ringing to prayers, and some of us have such a fancy for him that we stop our work so as to offer our devotions along with his.

"We do not know what to make of the lad, whether to laugh over him or cry over him. So we do both. Sometimes we laugh. . . . About three months before he became rector, he got married, and his courtship was fair comedy. You see, Mr. Charles

79

Danvers, a gentleman of noble fortune, did so much affect Mr. Herbert that he often publicly declared a desire that Mr. Herbert would marry one of his nine daughters: but he preferred it might be Jane, his favorite. Then Mr. Danvers talked so much to Jane about Mr. Herbert that she fell in love with him unseen. When she finally did meet him, she changed her name to Herbert in three days!

"At that time, three months before Mr. Herbert became our rector, he was not a minister at all, but a gentleman of the court. Then overnight, he put his ruffles away forever, and came home in a priest's garments. We laugh on every memory of the way he thereupon admonished his bride: 'You must now remember I have changed my sword and silk for a canonical coat, and you are now a minister's wife. You must from this time so far forget your father's place as not to claim precedence over any of your flock. A priest's wife can claim no first place but that which she purchases with her obliging humility.'

"And we laugh, too, at the way the bride parried her husband's startling announcement. The little dear, in sweet humility, dropt her long eye lashes, and with just a flicker of a smile replied that 'this was no vexing news to her: and he should see her observe it with cheerful willingness.'

"When she so responded, she destroyed at a blow his canonical dignity, and he thereupon did just what you would expect any sensible man to do under the circumstances.

"But we do not laugh when we see this young couple, both of noble birth, tending the flock day and night just as if they were born among us. . . . We love her just as we love him. They're a bonny couple. He has no mind at all for bookkeeping. He said in his sermon, 'A tithe purloin'd cankers the whole estate: and that goes for ministers too.' So he charged her with distributing their tithe. Bless her! She always over-spends it on the poor, then listens in mock humility when he with pretended sternness calls her to account.

"We smile at his big words when he preaches (O, he's such a scholar!). How he hammers those big words in with his long arms, like an actor! But we weep when we remember how devoted he is. When he took this church, he went alone (as the law requires) into the church to ring the bell. He was over long in coming out, so one of us slipped in, and there was Mr. Herbert on his face before the altar, weeping and crying 'O God, make me a good shepherd like the Lord Jesus Christ, my Master.' We laugh over Mr. Herbert and we love him. He's so genuine. He even writes love poems to God! And he never mentions Christ without saying immediately, 'My Master.' We've taken to calling the church bell, 'Mr. Herbert's Saint's - Bell.'

"Once he said in his sermon, 'Kneeling n'er spoiled silk stocking, so when the bell rings, seal up both thine eyes, and send them to thine heart that they may there spy out sins, and weep out the stains which by those sins arise.' What you have seen, sir, is what always happens when 'Mr. Herbert's Saint's - Bell' rings. We love him so much, we want to pray with him."

*   *   *

For over three hundred years "Mr. Herbert's Saint's-Bell" has continued to ring; and, at the sound of it, thousands of souls throughout the world have "turned delight into a sacrifice." George Herbert, like Robert Murray M'Cheyne, was the pastor of his little church but three short years. Isaac Walton wrote: "His sermons were so few!" Like M'Cheyne, Herbert died of tuberculosis. In March, 1663, at less than forty years, Herbert went to be with "His Master." M'Cheyne's Dundee was a tiny city almost under the shadows of the North Pole; and Herbert's Bemerton was a wee hamlet in the Avon Valley a mile from the little city of Salisbury. Yet each of these by-places has become a shrine of faith. It makes the heart stand still in contemplation of the supersonic quality of Saint's-Bell, enabling it to transcend the boundaries of time and space.

There now, this vignette is well along, and scarcely a word said about Herbert's being a top-shelf English poet. The only excuse we can offer is that Herbert's poetry was casual to Herbert. His poetry was made memorable by his life; not his life by his poetry.

Herbert's poems have high prominence in English literature. Here in Cedar-Palms there is an old edition of Herbert's, *The Temple,* printed in Boston, 1842. On the title page are these words in diamond type:

"Of the long and splendid line of British poets, from the earliest days down to Byron and Moore, there have been only some half dozen writers smit with the love of sacred song, whose genius was kindled at the altar of Christian devotion."

It is delightful to find how highly Lord Bacon esteemed Herbert's genius, and that a host of men of letters, like Richard Cranshaw, were indebted to him. William Cowper, "in chronic dejection of spirit, at length met with Herbert's poems; and Gothic and uncouth as they were, he yet found in them a strain of poetry which he could not but admire."

That is to say, Cowper's melancholia was ministered to by Herbert's sonnets, crude though they were! And that says it, just as I have been trying to say it; the beauty of Herbert's poetry was Herbert himself.

Well, Mr. Cowper, it's too bad there is no record that you ever inquired how Mr. Herbert's stumbling Gothic so blessed you. Had you taken the time you would have found just what the farmers found in Avon Valley. Every page of Herbert's poetry has

Saint's-Bell ringing in it. It was not the author's poems, but the author's piety that moved you.

*   *   *

This literary immortality, independent of rhyme and rhythm, came to Herbert's poetry by reason of an early resolve. At the age of seventeen, he wrote a letter to his mother:

"I . . . reprove the vanity of those many love-poems that are daily writ and consecrated to Venus . . . bewail that so few are writ that look towards God and heaven. For my own part, my meaning, dear mother, is, in these sonnets to declare my resolution to be, that my poor abilities shall be all and ever consecrated to God's poetry."

In this letter he enclosed a sonnet written for his mother, which began with a line that Spurgeon often quoted,

"O God, where is the ancient heat towards Thee
Wherewith whole shoals of martyrs once did burn?"

And there is Herbert's hiding of power. With a man of this sort, whether he writes or labors at a bench, whether he lives or is long since dead, his Saint's-Bell never ceases to ring.

*   *   *

George Herbert has often come into the study of Cedar-Palms to admonish me: "Please! Tell your readers that whatever of good there was in me was all of Grace. If I have been a beacon light, it's a borrowed glow!"

To comply with Mr. Herbert's wish, it is necessary to record swiftly his gentle birth, blameless life, winsome person, magnificent scholarship; then display how these blandishments had as little to do in *equipping* him for God's service as Hambleton's buffoon past in *preventing* him. Izaac Walton (that's right; author of the *Compleat Angler*) wrote a biography of George Herbert so factual that to this day it is the final life. One can't read Walton without talking like him:

Therefore, I can no longer hold back from my readers a knowledge of Herbert's advantage and natural goodness, and then display how, in the judgment of Herbert himself, these were inferior qualifications for his enablement.

*   *   *

On the third day of April, 1593, our subject was born to the noble family of Herbert, in "a plentiful castle on a plentiful estate." That castle stood near the village of Montgomery in Wales, where the Severn River flows out of the Welsh mountains into the Birmingham Plains. We cannot speak at length of his first twelve years, "a childhood in a sweet content"; of his pretty behavior, shining wit, and natural piety, which continued to the end. Nor can we linger upon his brilliant career as a Cambridge student, ending in his appointment as "Orator of the University."

Nor may we use much detail about his twelve years of success as orator. A university orator seems to be a sort of public relations man, with the function of Rotary Club chairman thrown in, especially on giving welcome addresses to the visiting notables. Herbert thus addressed James I—God save him!— when he visited Cambridge, and the Dandified Sovereign (See Scott's *The Fortunes of Nigel*) was so flattered that he "ended Herbert's progress in Cambridge and brought him into court."

Neither may we supply details as to Herbert's brilliant success in court, which was suddenly ended by the death of James. "In the year that Uzziah died," Herbert saw the Lord. With court gates closed, he decided to enter the ministry to which he had been greatly attracted during all his thirty-seven years.

Almost immediately he was offered "the pleasant rectory in the good air of Bemerton." But he esteemed himself unworthy, and delayed action certain days in deciding. Thereupon, Laud, Bishop of London, afterwards Archbishop of Canterbury, "became impatient over such dilly-dallying," made a hurried visit to see Herbert, "and did so convince Mr. Herbert that day that a tailor was sent for to come speedily to take measure and make him canonical clothes; which he did; and that same day, Herbert changed his sword and silk for a rector's gown!"

* * *

Being certain you do now love Mr. Herbert, we cannot hold back telling you how he looked and acted. Physically, he was too tall and thin to appear well in athletic garments; but by the same token, he looked uncommonly well in canonical blacks or court silks. He *knew* this, too; and had in both cases a good store in his wardrobes. His philosophy on this point was:

"Let thy mind's sweetness have his operation
Upon thy body, clothes and person."

If you were at all acquainted with the somewhat discredited science of physiognomy, you would note at once his lips were strangers to passion and intimates to prayer. He had so loving and meek a manner that gentlemen fell in love with him and his discourse; "and would contrive to meet him when he walked to Salisbury, or back to Bemerton." Afterward, they affirmed they had walked with a gentle saint from heaven.

* * *

We have no criticism for the farmers of Bemerton who were puzzled as to whether they should laugh over Mr. Herbert or love him. We do both. But we laugh at him because we love him, and we love him because we laugh at him.

* * *

When he lay dying, he handed to a friend the poems which he had written during his short life. These were published under the title *The Temple*. It is a choice book in Cedar-Palms; filled with wit and wisdom! We like to take it down for instance and read the end of a proud man:

> "Onely a herald, who that way does passe,
> Finds his crackt name at length in the Church glasse."

We esteem George Herbert our own chaplain. We read and re-read his lines of flaming love for Christ—"his Master"! For instance:

> "I have consider'd it, and finde
> There is no dealing with Thy mighty passion!
> For though I die for Thee, I am behind;
> My sinnes deserve the condemnation.
> Yet by confession will I come
> Unto Thy conquest. Though I can do nought
> Against Thee, in Thee will I overcome
> The man, who once against Thee fought."

Upon every reading of Herbert's poems, you will hear Saint's-Bell ringing again. Herbert's dust lies in little Bemerton, but some day, at Resurrection Morn, we expect to meet this gentleman of God and say, "We learned such a valued thing from thee, dear friend!

> "All must to their cold graves;
> But the religious actions of the just
> Smell sweet in death, and
> Blossom in the dust."

VII.

"BISHOP OF THIS WILDERNESS"

Francis Asbury

Rome is much awed by saints' relics. Protestants ought to pay more attention to such things. Deborah has one of Susannah's lace bobbins. I often pick it up and dream . . . "George," said Bishop Asbury, "where are your clothes?" "On my back, Bishop. I am ready at a moment's notice to go wherever you direct." I'd go a long way to see the needle by means of which George kept his garments together as he preached in the wilderness. (*Sketch Book*)

"BISHOP OF THIS WILDERNESS"

Francis Asbury

IT IS not prudent to write much about the thousands of miles we have driven over eastern United States, save to suggest that these journeys have woven a goodly part of life's weft. Deborah's map, marked in red, makes America appear to lie beneath crimson gauze. We can visualize it all, from the Everglades Crossing to the Boston Post Road; from Maine's little Frenchville on Number One to the Carolina swamps. The memories of such wayfaring constitute the treasury of things upon which men live after St. Martin's Summer has despoiled them.

And what do you think is uppermost when rainy nights spread out the map? The swanky apartments, all of a height, stretching northward forever from Central Park? The Tennessee Knobs where ginseng still rewards sharp eyes? Loblolly Pines drooping like canopies over Negro shacks? Quaint villages along the White Mountains? Of course. But the choicest tissue of dreams has been to think of the evangelizing great hearts who braved these areas when they still resounded to the howl of the wolf, and the woman-scream of the panther. Finney and the Tennants! Whitefield and Brainerd! There they went ahead of us—Hull in Georgia, Orange Scott in New England, Martin Rutter in Kentucky, Bascom in the Deep South, John Collins in Ohio, James Russell in the Carolinas, Stephen Olin in Connecticut, and—bless his old German heart—Jacob Gruber, Webber and Fields in one bundle, gloriously clowning for God in the early solitude. And we risk a storm of disagreement in affirming Francis Asbury was *facile princeps* of them all—the Bishop of the Church in this Wilderness!

*   *   *

Many have tried to get Francis into a phrase, but the ultimate—belonging to him and to him alone—first appeared in a letter dated from New York City in the year 1768. It was penned and sanded by one Thomas Taylor, and addressed to John Wesley; an importunate cry from early Methodism for "a man (preacher) of wisdom, of sound faith, and a *good disciplinarian* (italics mine) . . . one whose heart and soul are in the work . . . and I doubt not by the goodness of God such a flame will soon be kindled and would never stop until it reached the

Great South Sea (sic)!" Then the letter ended: "I
most earnestly beg an interest in your prayers, and
trust you will not forget the Church in this Wilderness."

Well, Mr. Taylor, that did it! You wanted "a
good disciplinarian," so God sent American Methodism its Man on Horseback—Francis Asbury, Bishop
of this Wilderness. And it is pleasing, friend Augus-
tus Lukeman, that before you died you took time off
from carving colossals in Pittsburgh and Montreal
to make a pair of sub-heroic equestrians of Asbury;
one for Washington, D. C., and one for Drew Theological Seminary; both much alike save that, in the
Washington statue, good old Spark had his head lower,
likely to dislodge an annoying Potomac horse fly.
And we thoroughly like what we find on the pedestal
of the Washington statue:

> "If you seek for the results of his labors,
> You will find them
> In our American civilization."

* * *

John Wesley did not forget the Church in this
Wilderness. Three years later, August, 1771, at the
Annual Conference in Bristol, England, the aging
Wesley "carried the matter to the floor." Silence fell
as the venerable saint, now at seventy, lifted his hand
and said, "Our brethren in America call aloud for
help!" (Long pause, then a passionate cry.) "Who

will go for us?" A young Briton of twenty-six—
that's right, our Francis Asbury—stood up. And
somebody ought to paint *that* picture on the walls
of the Boston Library right over some of the stuff
that's now there!

*   *   *

We can no longer hold back information about
our hero and his early life. Pin a map of England on
the wall through Birmingham and you have a fairly
balanced pin wheel. Four miles northwest of Birmingham the Hampstead Bridge crosses the Tame,
in a countryside fair enough to attract the estates
of wealthy gentlemen. Two such estates, in the year
1745, were jointly employing a gardener y-clept
Joseph Asbury, who pieced out his income with a
little truck garden of his own. Joseph and Elizabeth,
his wife, lived in an old stone house which had three
dormers, two big chimneys and a kitchen push-to.
In the earlier years of their marriage Elizabeth constantly grieved over her first born, Sarah, who died
in infancy.

A son named Thomas was born to Joseph Asbury
by a previous marriage. But Thomas was entirely
unlike his half-brother, Francis. Thomas was "an
avowed infidel and an abandoned sinner." He emigrated to Virginia. Among his descendants appeared
one Herbert Asbury, who published a biography of

his great-great-great Uncle Francis, *A Methodist Saint (Life of Bishop Asbury)*. The most striking thing about this *Life* is that one feels he is again hearing Thomas Asbury's assaults against the Faith once delivered.

* * *

"On August 20 or 21" 1745, Francis Asbury, the second and last child of Joseph and Elizabeth, was born in the old stone house. (How did it happen there was no adequate duocentennial in 1945?) Not long afterward, the Asburys moved to another home, in Great Barr, where his mother continued in grief over "her lovely baby." Francis remembered her as a stricken woman, "often standing by a large window poring over a book for hours together." (*The Asbury Journal*) She found Christ and peace when the Wesley revival caught up with her and, thereafter "for fifty years her hands, her house, her heart were open to receive the ministers of Christ." (*The Journal*)

Naturally, this kind of a home shaped the growing-up boy. From a child he "neither dared an oath nor hazarded a lie . . . abhorred mischief and wickedness." One of his mother's house guests, "a pious minister" began the good work in Francis, so that he was saved before he was fourteen. At once he began to "pray apart," particularly in a ramshackle old barn at Great Barr. Village wags said "it was kept together by the prayers of Young Asbury." There in the old barn on a memorable day, Francis got The Ancient Fire! "The Lord pardoned my sins and justified my soul."

He was at that time apprenticed to a blacksmith. (Please do not argue—there's an anvil on exhibition in England upon which he beat the iron.) But at leisure times, he began also to "testify" in homes. . . . His progress was rapid: "local preacher visiting regularly four of the nearby shires four or five times a week, for the sake of precious souls . . . at twenty he gave himself up to God and His work, after acting as a local preacher for near the space of five years."

*   *   *

That brings us up to the Bristol Conference, August 1771. . . . September 3, 1771, Francis Asbury embarked for "this Wilderness." A few days out at sea on the two month voyage to America, he wrote in *The Journal*:

"I will set down a few things that lie on my mind. Whither am I going?

"To the New World. What to do? To gain honor? No, if I know my own heart.

"To get money? No, I AM GOING TO LIVE TO GOD, AND BRING OTHERS SO TO DO." (Caps mine).

Day by day, while at sea, young Ashbury put his back to the Big Mast and preached to the passengers. October 27, 1771, he arrived in Philadelphia, "rented no room," almost immediately equipped himself with "saddle bags and one" (one horse), and began what Methodists delight to call "The Lónely Road." There the Lone Figure rode the wilderness horseback to the glory of God, in all one hundred and seventy-five thousand miles; twenty-five thousand miles more in a carriage after he became such an one as Paul the aged. Asbury, fearful that people would never believe he traveled so far, says in Volume II of *The Journal,* "I am recording the names of people with whom I stayed, so that my record may be verified."

*　　*　　*

Get on any fast train out of New York City, going any direction, and let the clicking rails tell you (whisper as you read):

Here's where Asbury preached,
   Asbury preached! Asbury preached!
Chester, Rye; West Farms, Amboy!
   Asbury preached! Asbury preached!
Wilmington, New Castle; Trenton and Bristol,
Haddonfield, Bloomingdale; Newton and Glouster,
Richmond, Savannah, Bost and Bangor:
   Asbury preached! Asbury preached!

(*Sketch Book*)

But he didn't get there on fast trains. He rode the wilderness on Jane or Fox, Panther or Charger. These horses grew old and died. When Spark was too infirm to go further, she broke Francis' heart by "nickering after him when he left her." (*The Journal*)

On December 25, 1784, Asbury was made Bishop of the newly-formed "Methodist Episcopal Church in America." But he continued to ride; the sort of bishop who was never addressed as "my Lord, having no splendid palace, no magnificent cathedral, no snug diocese; separating himself from all the comforts of life for sixty dollars a year, plunging into the wilderness to seek for lost sheep, preaching in barns, on stumps of trees, scorched by suns, bitten by driving snows, swimming vast rivers. . . ." (*North American Review*, 1862, Vol. 94, page 44)

Twenty thousand passionate sermons on salvation by grace and personal holiness! Where today will you find his successors? Ezra Squire Tipple, in *Francis Asbury*, writes mournfully but politely, "Asbury's sons in the gospel have grown to be milder mannered men."

*   *   *

The record of Francis' wilderness wayfaring clutches at your heart. Had it appeared at the same time as *Trader Horn*, it would have been the Book of the Month Club selection. If I had my way, Asbury's three-volume journal would be required reading for every young seminarian. Being now at the age where one is not easily stormed by any book, my heart nevertheless gets a powerful storming, feels a sharp sense of holy reproof, as I read *The Journal*:

> "I have not been many times more weary in my life . . ."
> "hard on the flesh to ride twenty miles every day and perform the duties of my station . . ."
> "very low in spirit . . ."
> "rode in great anguish. . . ."

You hear the honk of passing geese high above . . . you pause a moment with him to marvel over Niagara, or the glory of the west side of the Alleghenies. You are happy when a wilderness woman gives him "a fine piece of cherry pie." You are plenty mad when some cabin-boor refuses hospitality—and the next cabin twenty miles away! You wait for the main event of each day, when he opens the Book and speaks of the Saving Blood and Personal Holiness! Forty-five years of that! Twenty thousand sermons! Two hundred thousand miles of wayfaring for the Church in this Wilderness.

But when he began, American Methodism had less than seven hundred members, and less than ten preachers; and when, March 31, 1816, in the home of George Arnold near Fredericksburg, he smiled, lifted his hand (Saints'-Signal to Jesus) and died—

there were over 200,000 members, and seven hundred preachers.

*   *   *

Time fails to speak of his education, save to say that so far as formal education goes he didn't have much. But there are a lot of things you never learn in school. Had John Ruskin passed opinion on Asbury's circulating library in his saddle bag (four books on a trip) and the wilderness hours when he read the great books of his day (still the great books of ours)—*Pilgrim's Progress,* Baxter's *Call, Life of Brainerd* and the like; could Ruskin have heard him as he sang out Hebrew tones in the forests, or marked the points on Panther's saddle; heard how he kept on until he was *good* at Latin and *good* at Greek— Ruskin would have said, "Oxford could have added no more to him." Gruber, in his German accent, summed it up when he analyzed Swamp University: "We old ones tell the young ones all we know, and they try to tell the people all they can, and *they keep on trying until they can* — that's our college." It's plenty good.

*   *   *

Time fails also to speak much of Asbury the man—his five foot six body which riding kept at a good ring-side weight of one hundred and fifty; his warm-cold gray eyes (warm if you were right; cold if you were up to something). There were those who liked him not. In general they were up to something. "No woman would have him!" Well, reader, the Sketch Book has ten times as much material as this vignette, and it reveals *that* wasn't *the* reason he never married. He didn't feel it was right to drag a woman along with him, although there were plenty who would have liked it—with Asbury!

Some thought he was a martinet. I'm certain he was! I inquired of Julian C. McPheeters, President of Asbury Seminary (which, by the way, shares the honor with Asbury College of being the only American schools to bear his name), "Isn't there great danger in a Church hierarchy?" "Not if it's *right* at the top," replied the President. "But what if it isn't right at the top?" The President did not answer that one. He's a worthy Asbury successor.

* * *

Anyway, I have come to admire *good* martinets. I've just written *Breakfast Table Autocrat*, and wish again to emphasize, "Autocracy is sublimated if tempered to the will of God."

But—*the autocrat must make certain what God says; believe what His Book affirms; do what He wants done! Otherwise—!*

VIII.

A SON OF CRISPIN

William Carey

Rev. Sydney Smyth, one time canon of St. Paul's, toyed so much with a certain sharp weapon called wit that his only distinctive memoribilia is an anthology of clever statements made at the expense of others. When he came to Carey, he attempted to set the world laughing by the title, "Consecrated Cobbler!" Carey picked up the contemptuous phrase and wore it like a crown:

"Yes! A cobbler by the Grace of God!"

(Sketch Book)

A SON OF CRISPIN

William Carey

IT WOULD be regrettable should any conclude these vignettes were designed to trade upon stories of men who began in lowly walks, then became lustrous paragons. No! The wonder continuously under view then is that God selects men without regard to their advantage or disadvantage. Thus Paul the Scholar is of a kind, under grace, with Moorhouse of Auction Block Seminary. The wonder we have had in mind is the splendor with which God irradiates all men—"the same Lord *over all* who is rich *unto all* that call upon Him."

Of course, it is a pleasing secondary to mark how William Carey arose from a shoemaker's bench and took the high seat in the Translator's House. And Carey "just a cobbler!" We swiftly apologize for writing, "just a cobbler," because of a storm of protest. No workmen of any trade have been so proud of their business as the followers of "The Gentle

Craft." They will tell you, "This honorable title, *The Gentle Craft,* is given to no other occupation but that of shoemakers, and is an indication of the high esteem in which the Craft is held."

Of course! And we apologize. Were not the Saints Anianus, Hugh, Winfrid, and Crispinian *coblers?* And are not all cobblers since early days called "Sons of Crispin," Crispinian's brother, both of them fiery martyrs who preached as they made shoes? And while we are righting our slip of the pen, let's mention others who began with an awl in their hands: Shovell, and half a doen other admirals! Bradburn, head of the Wesley Conference! Coppelini, the painter; Bennet, the Rhymer; and Fox, the Quakerhead! Kitto, easily first in Palestinian geography! The good, grey poet, Whittier! . . . Let us make amends by suggesting that the proper line for grouping all people who out of weakness were made strong is:

> "The people that know their God
> Shall be strong and do exploits."

Nevertheless, ye Sons of the Leathern Apron, we shall never suppress our sense of delight in dreaming how William Carey overnight arose from the cobbler's bench and became "that myriad-minded man, at home in twenty-eight languages;" that shoemaker who, while tapping his pegs, resolved: "I shall always be poor until the Bible is publishing in Bengali and Hindustani." Before the world could realize it, Carey came forth with two Bibles, as complicated as Sanskrit —one in Bengali and one in Hindustani. Friends of The Gentle Craft, please do not be provoked: Carey's Progress is of the highest romance; it imparts divine heartburn just to think about it.

*　　*　　*

One of these vignettes suggested that, if Moody Bible Institute were explored to the headwaters, we would find an inspired auctioneer. Now, without subtlety, we affirm that if the vast modern missionary enterprise were tracked to its *ursprung*, we would come to a man on a shoemaker's bench. You would watch this Son of Crispin organize a foreign missionary society, then go out as that society's first missionary. You would see him for nearly thirty years Professor of Oriental Languages in the Marquis of Wellesly's pet project—the college which he founded at Fort William, India. You would watch Carey for a period of forty years building grammars—Mahratta, Sanskrit, Punjabi, Telugu, Bengali and Bhutani!— making and editing two dozen translations of the Bible, then putting these translations to press in his own Serampore book shop! Moreover, printing two hundred thousand Bibles in forty Oriental languages and dialects; plus hundreds of tracts and books in various languages! If you can bear more information, you ought to know that, in all this labor, Carey himself toiled in his shop in tasks all the way from printer's devil to entre-preneur.

That canny Cardiffian, William Edward Winks, wrote (1882): "It may be questioned if more work of a solid and useful character was ever pressed into one human life." You must listen respectfully when Winks generalizes. His own technique of research made Froissart look like a sophomore investigator. Just think! All of these achievements, and Mr. Carey "only a cobbler!"

*   *   *

We admit the foregoing is a good specimen of violating the canons of sequence; starting off with a peroration of a man's achievements without having him duly born and brought up. But the fact, Mr. Reader, that you have followed right along seems to indicate the violation was not a calamity, and that you will now have an improved interest in our subject's salad days.

We shuffle the calendar back to August 17, 1761, having led you up to the tiny English village of Pury, Northhampshire. We stop long enough to note that Pury is not a great distance from Frotheringay Castle where poor Queen Mary lost her head. And the great herds, scattered about on the fertile fields, confirm

that you are in The Milk Bowl of England. . . .
Over there is a Cottage of Excitement this seven-
teenth day of August, 1761, for a certain parish clerk
and school master, one Mr. Carey, has just become
a father! Since "William" had been a name service-
able enough for some of Prof. Carey's forebears, he
passed it on to the baby. Just "William Carey"—
like "Abraham Lincoln." Likely it never occurred
to the young father that the baby might need
a more impressive name, like "William Towcester
Carey."

At any rate, we have now properly launched William Carey; and need but little space to speak of
his education. He didn't have much to talk about.
Nor is there need of detail upon his being apprenticed
to a boot-maker while still in his teens. . . . Certainly
we ought not dwell on his twenty-five years of
wedded life—"married to a shrew old enough to be
his mother!"

If you feel like grieving over this, it might help
to remember that not every man finds his Joan on
the first try, and that men are not necessarily wrecked
by mesalliance. Look at Puritan Hooker! And
poor Moliere, wedded to a lady more vain than his
dramatic puppets; or John Wesley, whose wife walked
out on him in four weeks! It could be that Carey's
trials in trying to transform his wife into a sensible
woman not only made a student out of him but was

just the training needed for making the Hard Shell Baptists of the Eighteenth Century missionary-minded. It may be, also, that it will fall to some future Baptist to persuade certain contemporary Baptists to quit flirting with apostasy, because that deliverer has a wife named Jezebel.

*   *   *

During Mr. Carey's days at the bench, his mind was never pegged down with his awls, nor was his main concern the shoes he was making. Some one said, likely his employer, "Will never made a *pair* of shoes; he was too interested in Greek and Latin grammars." . . . As a small boy he was so fascinated with books on natural history that his bedroom looked like a museum; as a youth, he was described as a typical, bright, active, good-looking, intelligent British boy. In his maturity he was a little on the heavy side; long straight nose; mouth slightly pursed, as if about to say "prism"; eyes wide apart and calm, with a notable space above his brows before you reached the receding hair line. You could easily imagine him, with his white frilly collar above his dark vest, as one of the signers of the Declaration of Independence.

*   *   *

In later years, after Carey had become the world's number one linguist, good old Rev. Thomas Scott

would pause at the door of the little shoe shop, brush
a tear aside and say, "This was Mr. Carey's college."
It is easy to pardon Brother Scott for being tearful
over anything pertaining to Carey. Was it not under
Scott's preaching in the little village church that
Carey came to Jesus? And, equally important, did
not Scott make a Baptist out of Carey? Further,
was not Carey's mental gianthood a product of regen-
eration, "that vital change of heart," (the old
preacher was wont to say) "which lays the foundations of excellence; never a school of learning"? Then,
as if to drive his three prong exaltion home, he
would lean against the door posts and say, "This was
Mr. Carey's college."

*   *   *

From here on — from Carey's conversion — our
narrative takes wings. Uniting with the church at
twenty-two, he became pastor of the tiny Baptist
Church at Moulton at twenty-five, piecing out a
miserable income with shoe leather; "once a fortnight, Carey might be seen walking eight or ten
miles to Northampton, with his wallet full of shoes
on his shoulder, and returning home with a fresh
supply of leather." But there is no need to feel
sorry for him. The finest aid in the world for making a sermon outline is a long walk up the Brook
Kidron.

During the Moulton pastorate, Carey began the practice of *"alloting his time and sticking to the allotment."* During this period also he sharpened his face by fellowship with such men as John Suttclife, and the father of the eloquent Robert Hall, and Andrew Fuller. Fuller heard Carey in a short address at a Baptist Association. Perhaps it was "a Devotional," programmers' favorite way of taking care of lesser fry without damage to the time of the "main speakers." Fuller was so charmed with Carey's piety and wisdom that a life-long friendship forthwith began; "a friendship of untold blessing to the heathen."

Likely it was at Moulton that Carey first came across Captain Cook's account of his voyage around the world. As he read Cook's volume, he hung a large map on the wall, and traced Cook's progress. This proved to be Carey's undoing—his heart took fire in behalf of "the heathen without the gospel"; worked him up to such an extent that he began to irritate Baptist Associations on the subject of missions; finally got to himself a withering rebuke from an old Baptist Bellwether who, in effect, told Carey to sit down and shut up: "Young man, sit down; when God pleases to convert the heathen, he will do it without your aid or mine." (This indignation technique is last ditch fighting, and will never be abandoned. In our generation, it first grows eloquent on "Co-opie-ration," then perorates on the dangers of leadership without formal education.)

* * *

One of Carey's pamphlets introduced a slogan that will outlive the best in modern commercial advertising:

> "Expect great things from God,
> Attempt great things for God."

He read this pamphlet before a Baptist Association. They listened to him, were impressed somewhat, and went right on to adjourn the meeting. Carey seized Fuller's hand in an agony of distress and tearfully pleaded, "Do something now!" So—they passed a resolution: "They resolved on this holy enterprise."

* * *

One never thinks much of resolutions. No futility is so dreadful as to be named on the Resolutions Committee. It is melancholy to think of an afternoon's work buried behind a motion to adjourn. But that resolution had a better experience. In May 1792, "a society was formed." Thereupon followed a fiery sequence of meetings, committees, travels, labors, deputations and—disappointments. In the Autumn of 1792 the first offering was taken, amounting to $65.72. "And that offering was the forerunner of the subsequent millions given to convey the message of salvation to the heathen!" On the 9th of January,

1783, Carey and a colleague sailed to India. Carey, like Asbury, had a one-way ticket; he never returned on furlough or participated in "health-building ocean voyages."

Long ago we heard of a poor German novelist who, alas, ran out of writing paper with his hero no further than the middle of the bridge. Of this bitterness we share, and never tire of citing the incident. We know just how that author suffered. Thus, with the curtain descending on the Carey vignette, we hasten to make one more reference.

*   *   *

Small souls, like Sydney Smyth, have lifted the lip against the epitaph which Carey wished carved upon his own tomb:

William Carey
Born August 1761   Died June 1834
"A wretched, poor, and helpless worm,
On Thy kind arms I fall."

But we do not lift the lip! Our eyes become fountains. That sentiment was sincerity and genuine piety. "And this was the base of all his excellence." He never took credit for anything but plodding. And God took his plodding and overspread it with His glory.

IX.

SO THEY CALLED HIS NAME
CHRISTMAS

Christmas Evans

Oh, my soul, thou hast but to note how our Sovereign Lord answers the prayers of His servants. A lingering death must be hard! This day I have noted how Christmas, while yet 'twas day, filed his petition for an easy departure:

"XI. Take upon Thyself, O Jesus, to prepare me for death, for Thou art God; and Thou needest but to speak the word. If it be possible—but Thy will be done—let me not linger in sickness, nor die a sudden death without bidding adieu to my brethren, but rather let me die with them around me, after a short illness. May everything be put in order for that day of passing from one world to another, so that there may be no confusion or disorder, but a passing in peace. O grant me this for the sake of Thine agony in the garden. Amen. — C. E."

Even so, Lord Jesus, do Thou remember Thy servant!

(Sketch Book)

SO THEY CALLED HIS NAME
CHRISTMAS

Christmas Evans

W HEN you open the pages of Welsh literature, a weird set of place-and-person names pop right
out at you—Dyfrig, Llanwenarth, Brycheiniawg and
Dhu of Hiraddug. "When did Welshmen get that
way?" one muses; and the answer is, They were always that way, ever since the mysterious Brythons
emigrated from Amorica, mixed it up, language and
all, with the Goidals and Ivernians and emerged as
Welshmen, speaking a nervous, bony, muscular
tongue called Welsh. Romans in the early A.D. days
were amused by reports from foreign service armies
—"Cunnedda Wledig is giving trouble; Maelwynawg
ab Tudwal heads up Welsh chieftains." . . . Deborah
has a little cream pitcher which she purchased in
Porth. On the side of it is printed "Dydd Da." It
should be said, that Welsh spells harsher than it
sounds; and you can never find a sweeter way to say
"Good morning!" than "Dydd Da!"

Of course, one does find normal Welsh names from time to time. There was, for instance, a poor shoemaker named *Samuel Evans*(*!*) who with his wife *Joanna* lived at Ysargarwen, Parish of Llandysol, Cardiganshire. On December 25, 1766, the first-born came to the rubble cottage of the young Evans'. They thought of naming the baby "Vasover"; but it was Yuletide, so they called his name Christmas. You might not understand the soft vowels and stabbing consonants Mr. and Mrs. Evans used in talking to the baby. But you would hear, over and over a phrase you knew, "Christmas, bach!" ("Christmas, lad"!)

*   *   *

Naturally, the humble Evans cottage was a home of faith—"a Jesu Grist Te." The Welsh have had from the beginning a genius for Apostolic Christianity. No country has more vigorously resisted Roman Catholic superstitions, nor has any country paid more heavily for their resistance. Welsh martyrdoms are a chapter from world-wide Papal atrocities which, as Spurgeon says, should be kept fresh in mind "lest we give over utterly to Rome and the Devil." Herewith, then, we present a cameo record of Christianity in Wales, serving this vignette in two particulars; a brief of the faith which Christmas

Evans received from the very air he breathed; and, a
record of fidelity to that faith even unto death.

*   *   *

Christianity began in Wales when Claudia returned from Rome with her husband in the year 63
A.D. She had found Christ while listening to the
preaching of Paul in Roman bonds, and came back to
her homeland, Wales, with a heart on fire for God . . .
A hundred years later Faganus and Dominicanus,
also, were won to Christ while on a visit to Rome,
and returned to Wales, 178 A.D., "as able ministers
of Christ." They poured a torrent of fiery preaching against Druidism, and won to the faith its very
first king—Lucius, King of Wales. . . . One hundred and thirty years later another king, Constantine,
became a Christian (though a nominal one) largely
through his Welsh mother. But—as Welshmen say—
"Constantine opened the doors and the man of sin
seated himself in the Temple of God." Catholicism
forthwith initiated her expendiency plan for swiftly winning the world by incorporating gross superstitions and abuses into her worship. This the Welsh,
by reason of their Apostolic simplicity, instantly and
continuously resisted.

In the seventh century, Austin, gun-man for the
Vatican, arrived in Great Britain to make Papal prose-
lytes. He did well among the Saxons; but the Welsh,

being enlightened Christians, stood firm. This infuriated Austin. He instigated the Saxons to assault a Welsh Christian assembly. Twelve hundred ministers and delegates were slain, and Welsh believers "fled to the mountains of Cumry (Wales)." That was Rome when she could get away with it: and that is still Rome!

Catholic vitrol in passing years was continuously poured out on Wales. From 1658 to 1684 hundreds of Welsh Christians were ravaged, tortured and killed. However, persecution is the hot house which produces Christian prophets, so these times marked the appearance of such great Welsh preachers as Vasover, Powell and Roger Williams.

This peculiar Christian background produced equally curious results. E. Paxton Hood remarks that, in the mountains of Wales, the pulpit is everything: "therein the people find orchestra and stage; music, painting and acting all looked for and found in the preacher." The English gather their monster crowds for "the Darby": Wales awards hers to Gospel preaching. America touts her bond sales with movie actors; but Wales sends for a Protestant minister. Some one said, "You find no Ruskins or Carlyles in Wales." True! Such persons had no box office appeal to the Welshmen! They gave their premiums to their Walter Brutes and Davydd Ddus.

The Welsh language itself, despite the smiles with which we began, was heaven's gift to preaching. It is a tongue of rugged consonants married to gentle vowels—setting up housekeeping in outstanding sentences. These sentences one moment prod the mind with sharp goads, and the next comfort the heart with angelic lullabies. Welsh is so difficult that it is like a new motor car; you just can't run it fast unless you know what you're about. You can preach in English without thinking much; but to preach in Welsh you must first *feel* your message or you will not get words for it. . . . And—do Welshmen know how to sing! Gorgeous heaven-reaching *a cappella!* . . . Ah, reader o'mine, Wales is a good country for preaching! And a good country for preaching is a good country. Period.

*   *   *

The boy, Christmas, had other gifts not so easy to take. For one, he was born and raised in poverty. And everyone knows, who knows anything, that this rough tutor heads up the Egyptian College in which the heralds of God are refined. We are still looking for a good preacher who was brought up on a Persian rug.

When Christmas was nine, Samuel his father, died in his cobbler stall with his awl in his hand. For a short time, Joanna desperately tried to keep her little brood together; even "went on the county." But to no avail. The scattering of the children began. Christmas was sent to live with his farmer uncle, James Lewis. And Uncle Jim was a bad one — straight through and back again.

Christmas, in the next seven years, followed in his uncle's ragged footsteps; he ran with a gang of young mountain hoodlums. At seventeen, he and some others were awakened under the preaching of Rev. David Davies. The young converts met together in a barn at Penypralltfaus, poring over Bibles in the light of their candles: "thus in a month Evans was able to read the Bible in his mother tongue."

Thereupon he entertained ministerial ambitions, memorized another man's sermon, and still another man's prayer. Of this appropriation, he made no confession; became an overnight sensation—and a swift backslider! When he was "converted" (Luke 22:31) his self abasement was fathomless: he saw himself to be "a mass of ignorance."

His penitent return stirred up the wrath of his Apache friends. Six of them assaulted him with clubs one night as he made his way home on the mountain road from a church service. One blow landed on his forehead, destroyed his right eye and left him to the end of his days with "a ghastly empty socket."

The night following this heavy disaster Christmas dreamed: "I saw Jesus in the clouds, and all the world on fire. Jesus said, 'Thou thoughtest to be a preacher . . . it is too late'!" That did it! Although he still esteemed himself a mass of sin and ignorance, he set his feet in the long, lonely path of a prophet. . . . He preached for several years as invited. In 1790, at twenty-four, Christmas was ordained a Baptist minister at Lleyn, Caernarvonshire, and became pastor of his first church, same place. In 1790, also, he married Miss Catharine Jones.

*   *   *

Ah, good reader, Miss Catharine Jones! She was the Welsh version of Susannah Spurgeon! God never did a better thing for Christmas, after the new heart, than when He gave him Catharine, still in her teens. She was Dorcas, Ruth and Lydia of Thyatira all wrapped up in one adorable bundle. "She loved the Church and made all the interests of His Church her interests." She would, therefore, rather be Chirstmas' wife—on a salary that never exceeded $85.00 a year—than to be "the Prin-cess of Wales."

On five of Evans' evangelistic missions in Wales, through rain and sleet and snow, Catharine made the journey with him, horseback—right behind him on the same horse. Thus she continued, *right behind him* in everything, until her death thirty-four years later. Evans, then at sixty, wrote: " 'She has gone the way of all the earth.' . . . His tears nearly destroyed his remaining eye; he wondered how he escaped sinking into the grave. . . . But one comfort remained; in the pulpit he felt raised to Paradise — forgot his afflictions."

*   *   *

Christmas Day 1810 was memorable to Christmas and Catharine. Closing the Lleyn pastorate, after thirty years, they left, mounted on horseback (Catharine right behind him), no worldly goods, to assume a pastorate in the Isle of Angelsea. "It was a rough day of frost and snow, and we—like Abraham—knew not whither we went. But we did know Him who said, 'I am thy exceeding great reward'!"

Angelsea, a roundish island of one hundred and eighty-nine square miles, lies just off the northwest coast of Wales. There is very little timber, it is insipidly flat, marked by pea-soup Autumn fogs, and filled with multitudes of sheep. Even the sheep looked discontented. Packet boats run from Holyhead to Dublin; but who wants to go to Dublin? A five-minute bridge connects Angelsea with the mainland today; a twenty-minute ferry when Christmas and Catharine arrived.

*   *   *

For some impish reason, Christmas began his Angelsea ministry by abandoning the sweetness of the Gospel for the bitterness of controversy. He fashioned an armory of sermonic clubs against Sande-manianism (Calvinism gone to seed). Naturally the dew dried off Gilboa, as it does with preachers who major on the social gospel. His health failed, his ministerial joy departed, a deep nostalgia arose for the olden days which he knew in Lleyn. Therefore, in the second year of his Angelsea ministry, lacking a horse, he was obliged to leave Catharine behind. He set out on foot for South Wales "seeking what he had lost." As he passed through the mountain villages he preached, but no longer against Sandemanianism; "he preached Jesus only. His poor heart began to warm again."

One day, as he trudged between Dongelly and Machyulleth, climbing up towards Cadair Idris, "he had to pray. The struggle lasted for hours. Soon he felt the fetters loosening, his hard heart softening; his tears began to flow, his joy of salvation returning." In the preaching service next day, "he found his heart had removed from cold and sterile regions, into the verdant fields of God's presence. The Holy Ghost was working everywhere!"

Thus Evans, at forty-seven, entered a deeper experience. He immediately wrote down a thirteen itemed covenant with God, initialing every one of the thirteen. Two items are of great interest:

4. "Grant that I may not be left to any foolish act (such as anti-Sandemanianism) that may occasion my gifts to wither and be rendered useless before my life ends. (Signed) C. E."

8. "Grant that I may experience the power of Thy word *before* I deliver it, as Moses felt the power of his own rod before he saw it on the land and waters of Egypt. (Signed) C. E."

*   *   *

Some very excellent specimens of Evans' sermons may be found in Rev. Joseph Cross', *Sermons of Christmas Evans,* (Kenny and Sumner, Chicago, 1870). But those familiar with Welsh and English affirm 'you can scarcely recognize Evans sermons, translated into English, as the same discourses that this Gargantuan preacher delivered in Welsh."

*   *   *

"Gargantuan" is a good word for Evans. Contemporary writers who had a flair for strong-color words thus described Evans: "The tallest, stoutest, greatest man one ever saw. He appears like one composed, on the day after a great battle, out of the scattered members of the slain. An Anak whose head is covered with thick, coarse, black hair. His gait unwieldy, his limbs unequal. He has but one eye— if it might be called an eye—more properly, a brilliant star over against a ghastly empty socket." President Benajah Harvey Carroll, speaking to students in the Southwestern Baptist Theological Seminary, exclaimed, "But, my soul, he could preach! Gentlemen! Gentlemen! I would rather be able to preach to lost souls like Christmas Evans than to be the author of every speculative vagary since Epicurus died, and all the flimsy higher criticism that ever evidenced a palsied grasp on faith!"

Time fails to analyze Evans' sermons. You must do that for yourself. You will behold the naked demoniac bounding out of the tombs . . . see Jesus in the quiet of His majesty cast the demon out with a word . . . hear Evans describe how Paul pulled ancient sinners out of their graves and hung them as a warning over his pulpit. But even then you will miss how the throngs which heard Evans went wild; fell to the ground as if rocked by an earthquake.

*   *   *

Evans rode his horse, Jack, through Wales for twenty-seven years after his deeper experience, and the slain of the Lord fell everywhere. In barren mountains alone with Jack, Evans frequently talked to the horse. The animal became old in his master's service, knew at a distance his voice; lifted up his ears when Christmas began to speak: nickered back constantly as Evans spoke to Him on their solitary journeys.

Monday evening, July 14, 1838, Christmas hitched Jack at the rail in front of the Swansea Church, entered the building and mounted the pulpit stairs. Had you been present, weeping and rejoicing as Evans talked to the angel of Resurrection morn — "that wonderful messenger with a wonderful message"— you would have said, "Aye, but Gabriel couldn't preach as well as Christmas, for Gabriel didn't need salvation." After two hours he came down, desperately ill, and said in English, "This is my last sermon!"

It was. Once, in the closing moments, he exclaimed to the friends gathered about his bed, weeping, "Don't weep for me! Forty and eight years have I ministered in the Sanctuary. But I have never labored without blood in the basin."

Someone began to sing the old Welsh hymn, "Drive On." "Good bye!" he thereupon cried to the mourners. Then, as body and mind were dissolving, he thought himself once again in the Mountains of Cumry, astride Jack. "Drive on, Jack, bach! We have only to cross one low mountain, and then there will be oats, excellent water and a good stable. Drive on!" And the angels, of whom he spoke so much, conveyed him to the house not made with hands, eternal in the heavens; a house in every particular worthy of the shelter he desired for his beloved Jack.

X.

THE BOOKSELLER OF FINSBURY SQUARE

James Lackington

When the wealthy Mr. Lackington returned to his boyhood home, "the bells rang merrily all the day of his arrival . . . Some of the most respectable people were pleased to inform him that their reason for paying particular attention was that he did not so far forget himself as many proud upstarts have done: that the notice he took of his poor relations, and old acquaintance, merited the respect and approbation of every real gentlemen." (*Memoirs*)

THE BOOKSELLER OF
FINSBURY SQUARE

James Lackington

IF ANY reason appeared which obliged us
to leave Lofty Redwood Valley, it is assuasive to
remember there are other places in the world super-
lative for living: somewhere in the Connecticut Valley; summer at Taos; winter in Maricopa, or London
anytime—climaxing in the order named. You see,
the City of Picadilly Circus and Bethnal Green has the
strata of history so neatly piled that one may relive
any period he desires, from King Alfred to Charles
Spurgeon; from Queen Elizabeth to Number 10
Downing Street. . . . One memorable spring, for instance, we had a taste for Lord Mayors, so we frequently went into a little side street near the British
Museum where an old actor conducted a puppet
show—whensoever as many as two persons appeared
with a shilling apiece. His figurines, clanking around
on a low turn-table, were a bit seedy but perfectly

authentic. No one could criticize the mouse-sized horses, or the brave little carriages, no larger than ink wells. We watched diminutive soldiers march by, accompanied by rabble boys. . . . but we fairly gasped each time the climax came. The old actor, in his best Cheapside voice, pompously announced, "The Lawd May-yuh of Lun-dun!" There he was indeed—his diminutive Highness in a gorgeous, doily-sized, red greatcoat.

*   *   *

Now the function of the preceding paragraph is to make it appear perfectly natural to open the door of this vignette and invite you to walk into the year 1798, City of London, and take a position in Finsbury Square just opposite an enormous building on the corner. When the wind straightens out the large pennant floating above the corner tower, you read the ten-inch letters: "Temple of the Muses." You are amazed on being informed that this is the biggest book store in the world, though the sign above the m..in door reads: "The *Cheapest* Book Store in the World." In gold on the entrance glass are the words, "James Lackington."

James Lackington! Not one reader in a thousand will have ever heard of him, yet his career is a page out of The Romance of Christian Business, a seventy year demonstration that in the long run business men are successful because they are Christians, and Christians because they are successful. . . . Let us ascend the piled-up white arcs of scrubbed marble which form the front steps, and thus into "The Temple." The several floors of the building have been cut away, creating a series of galleries along the walls, rising in tiers to the dome. Books—tens of thousands of them! —soar in orderly flocks from the entrance level to the dome, the expensive ones on the bottom rows, the cheaper ones on the top. This is good going, for thus a customer's first impression is that of elegance, not dog-ears. Mr. Lackington will tell you (just to prove there are no really new jokes in the world), "The lower books are higher because they are lower; and the higher are lower because they are higher." His giant catalogs, scattered about on the first floor, claim "Half a million books constantly on sale!"

You say, amazed, "What! a book business like that in 1798?" That's right: and you might as well learn herewith that the proportions of modern book vending began with James Lackington. The gentlemen of Kingsport and the Shemisroils of the Fortnight Club may all be called "The Sons of Lackington." Any untempered remarks, therefore, about the amazing size of modern book sales sounds like a Johnstown survivor boasting in the presence of Noah.

*   *   *

However, you are looking not only upon a great eighteenth century book business, but also upon an enterprise that has powerfully influenced modern commerce. Here comes Mr. Lackington now—rich as he is, he is always on the job, his hand on everything, even to compiling the catalogs. Size him up carefully before he starts to speak: he is so witty, you will have time for naught else, once he starts. And by the way, remember "wit" is not primarily something funny. It is basically a startling combination of ideas, like "Our disappointments are God's appointments." That's real wit, and not a bit funny.

* * *

Mr. Lackington's hair is barbered long on the sides around the temples, then flaired out into ruffs. (Not bad, perhaps, for a man of fifty; but Gray Polls do well to go in for clippers.) His nose is long and straight. Eyes a bit large, and much too far apart. Jaws, somewhat porcine like the jowls of Edward (Roman Empire) Gibbons.

* * *

"Now, Mr. Lackington, have you anything to say to Modern Business?" (And Modern Business, from Five-and-Dime Stores to Porcelain-lined Hot Dog Stands, would do well to take notes.)

"Well, your modern business has already profited from my advice. (You see at once he is modest.) But I do not mind repeating.

"Keep your shop as clean as a pin. A clean shop imparts its allure to your wares—even second hand books. . . .

"Sell at the lowest price which will bear a working profit. Never over-price an article.

"Quick sales! Yesterday I bought $60,000.00 worth of old books and remainders in the London book sales. That means I must sell quickly or confer with the bailiff. Small profits on thousands of sales rather than large profits on a few.

"Buy recklessly, but wisely: sell bullishly but shrewdly. (*You work that one out yourself!*)

"Sell beneath the real value, and your customers will forget your competitors' address.

"Keep open books so that your employees may see how things are going. Anybody can see I cleared $50,000.00 last year. (Whew! that was a President's salary in America's Golden Days!) Because my men know what I make, and that there are no shady deals, they're proud of me. They also know my progress will be reflected in their pay bags.

"Reach for your cheque book and start writing the minute you get an invoice. Make your customers pay cash, and do it yourself. That may postpone the purchase of a new model coach and four. Folks may laugh at you, but they'll love to do business with you.

"In short, do business as a Christian gentleman should, and you'll always have a jingle in your old side-sporran!"

*   *   *

There are two records from which the materials for this vignette are drawn: H. Curwen's, *History of Booksellers*, which provides many a tasty currant for authors' cookies. And Lackington's own account of his life, *Memoirs and Confessions* (1826). You will be fortunate if you get either of them.

A man who decides to write and publish his autobiography is off on a Hotspur venture from which few return. The few that do survive are magnificent egotists who apparently never take themselves seriously, and are so clever about it that their readers end up infatuated with the clowning Meographers. The back thought here is that, when a man laughs at himself, the readers are spared the necessity. And Lackington's *Exit Laughing* is one of the ten great autobiographies.

*   *   *

He assumes he is a restaurateur in his book. The frontispiece is, of course, a likeness of himself, with this text: "A striking likeness of your cook." In the preface, he hopes his readers "will enjoy the feast with the same good humor with which he has prepared it." His forty-seven chapters are "dishes" which pro-rated on the book cost, are "two pence each"; that, naturally, makes his book a savory bargain. Then he adds, "Ladies and gentlemen, pray be seated and much good may it do you!"

What weapons of sarcasm may be forged against so beloved an egotist? He proceeds to tell you, naively, how his methods and principles first made booksellers furious, and how later *those who remained in business* adopted them! He lets you know that his profits have procured for him a town house, a country house, "a chariot," and a liveried James. Of course, some were jealous and talked scandalously; asserted "he found this money in an old book." To this he replies, "But of course! and I'll confess the name of the book, *Small Profits,* bound by Industry and clasped by Economy."

His enemies sneered that he was "only a poor shoe-maker." Of that he was proud: "The first King of Bohemia kept his country shoes by him to remind him from whence he was taken." . . . And, furthermore, he had much more pleasure while riding his carriage, thinking how he got it, than some he might mention if they remembered how they got theirs. Then, to cap his infamy, he had gold letters put on his carriage door:

"Small profits do Great Things."

Now what can you do with a man like that? There is no harm, therefore, in telling all about the humble beginnings of James Lackington.

* * *

He was born in a Quaker home, Wellington, Somersetshire, August 31, 1746. His father, an apprenticed shoemaker, romanced with a girl and married her when both were in their Bobby Sox Age. This so angered grandfather Lackington that he disinherited them. Joan, however, turned out to be such an adorable young mother, so industrious, affectionate and sweet, that grandfather relented and set Father up in a business of his own. Father Lackington thereupon wrecked himself on a new Rumpus Room and Bar, and moved his family into Poverty Row.

Here, then, we launch James Lackington — a drunkard's son, in abject poverty. He never had more than a few weeks education and that at "a dame school." Bound at fourteen to the Bowdens of Taunton, his horizon was limited to shoemaker's awls, stools, stalls, and hammers.

The Wesley Preachers came along, whom the Baptist Bowdens didn't like, and James was saved at sixteen. Along with salvation came mental awakening. He paid one of his employer's sons six cents a week to teach him to read. . . .

At twenty he was "freed"; but, alas, in the backwash of rejoicing he took a fling at blacksliding. . . .

Hearing John Wesley preach one memorable night in Broadmede Shapel "lighted again the old fire of religious enthusiasm." . . . At twenty-four he married "Nancy, a dairy maid whom he had loved for seven years . . . she was accounted handsome, was a devout Methodist, an amiable, industrious, thrifty woman." They were wretchedly poor when married: "After searching our pockets (which we did not do in a careless manner) we found but one half-penny to begin the world with." But they made a romance out of penury and often sang together with high glee Samuel Wesley's (father of John) amphibrach verses:

> "Those blessings which Providence kindly has lent,
> I'll justly and gratefully prize;
> While sweet meditation and cheerful content
> Shall make me both healthy and wise.
>
> "How vainly through infinite trouble and strife,
> The many their labors employ;
> While all that is truly delightful in life
> Is what all, if they will, may enjoy."

*   *   *

The young Lackingtons continued in abject poverty until they decided to move to London; they arrived "with half a crown between them." But the higher wages in the shoe business of the city caused them to prosper to such an extent that Lackington went into business for himself in his own little shoe shop. He did so well the first year that he "got a silk coat for Nancy and a great-coat for himself—

the first he ever had." Having a lively taste for books, he decided to carry a side line in his shoe shop: "He put in a few second-hand books so he would have plenty to read himself." Book sales almost immediately went so well that he abandoned cobbling and became a bookseller.

In the rising tide of prosperity, he moved his shop "right up Broadway"— in 1775, Featherstone Street; in 1776, Chiswell Street; and in 1792, Finsbury Square, occupying the vast old building which he refurbished colorfully and re-named, "The Temple of the Muses." His first year's profits were $25,000! By 1798, the year we are visiting the Temple, he had made a princely fortune, and at fifty-two was "retiring." It should be said that he had planned to retire at forty-seven, and had sufficient to go on; but he continued in business five years longer so as to finance his poor relations for the future, and *"to have more money for the Lord's work!"*

*   *   *

Lackington made England "book conscious." "Everybody reads! The poorest sort who had spent their evenings relating stories of hobgoblins, now read. You see *Pamela* and *Peregrine Pickle* on every table. Women even keep books on the bacon rack while they get breakfast ready." He did not conduct a Book of the Month Club — and dispose of "remainders" as premiums. He thought his plan was better. He would purchase ten thousand remainders in one order, then mark them down and sell them in a quick sale at the Temple. Once he bought up over ten thousand of Wesley's hymn books! But he sold them, and fast—and had London singing:

"Ye servants of God, your Master proclaim!
And publish abroad His wonderful name!"

You see, Charles could write gospel poetry, but it took a good bookseller to "publish it abroad."

*   *   *

Lackington's exceptional business romance was simply an eighteenth century version of a man who combined business sagacity and Christian idealism. When Lackington began in business, his sagacity was uppermost. As he grew in grace, his Christian idealism became uppermost. But, even at the beginning, he was not deficient in Christian idealism; nor was he lacking, to the very end, in business sagacity. He *slowly* added, as his wealth increased, sensible and "assimilable" comforts. Why should he ride to work across London in a stage when his own carriage was so much more comfortable?

His Christian stewardship, however, did not increase slowly — it leaped prodigally. Thousands of pounds went into chapel building; thousands to folks in need; thousands to "good ministers who didn't have good wages."

*   *   *

Well, Mr. Lackington, in this year 1798—when you are about to "retire"—what are you going to do?

Retirement is a feeble word for Lackington's last seventeen years. He was "on the go" more than ever. He went all over Great Britain. One of his pet jokes was to drive up to the old establishments where he once worked, alight from his splendid carriage and inquire of the shoemaker, "Sir, have you any occasion"? That was the formula for "Would you give me a job, sir?" After the consternation had passed, and they recognized him, everybody laughed; and "they were right glad to see me, everyone of them."

In his closing years, Lackington gave the bulk of his time to lay preaching, to calling upon the sick and destitute! He did not arrive in a privately owned Lockheed, but he did come in a jolly coach and four, with red-liveried lads on the high seat. I say, good friends, that was a toppin' way to retire, eh what?

*   *   *

He was buried in Budleigh Church Yard, in Budleigh Deeonshire, near his great estate. A simple shaft once marked the spot:

> "James Lackington
> Died 22 of Nov.
> in the 70 year of his age."

There is nothing this writer would more enjoy doing, if he could get permission, and if the monument still stands, than to have Lackington's own life motto carved on the marble:

"SUTOR ULTRA CREPIDAM FELICITU
AUSUS."

This being translated reads, "The shoemaker happily abandons his last." . . . We must add, on our own, "There is but one way a man may happily lay aside the tools of his livelihood—that is, if while yet 'tis day, he uses them as unto the Lord."

XI.

THE MAGNIFICENT ATAVIST

Dwight L. Moody

"Thus saith the Lord, Stand ye in the ways, and see, and ask for the old paths, where is the good way, and walk therein, and ye shall find rest for your souls." (*Jeremiah* 6:16)

THE MAGNIFICENT ATAVIST

Dwight L. Moody

A UNIVERSITY background makes one aware that there is a smell of fire on the word Atavism, and the business of lifting one's nose: "Reversion to primitive type: renewed manifestation of the characters peculiar to a remote ancestor, instead of those of an immediate or near one." And of course one fears to be an atavist if he is committed to the idea that "change means progress." But, alas! some of us, by reason of the decent necessity for hiding away in the kind darkness of woodshed rafters so many objects upon which our best tinkering has been lavished, have lost confidence in such a protasis.

Under such conditions, we sense a shamefaced hospitality towards—even Atavism! No small number of us have secret qualms over how well the contemporary Church with its "advanced approach," *hasn't been doing* in the past forty-five years. This leaves us pathetically exposed to a charge of heresy against "the assured results of progress."

There now! I was so fascinated that I nearly took a siding! But I will not do it again. That's a promise. I'll stick to Moody so closely that, if anyone is provoked, it will be D. L.'s fault, not mine. Just one mouse-like suggestion, and then we'll proceed where the course is open. To me, a son of the campus, it has brought a thrill quite up to my boyish emotions over *St. Nicholas Magazine,* to peep into *Orthodoxy's Memoirs,* there to observe how the Commoner of Northfield—going in for old methods, old ideas, and old ideals—moved the world! while I had been wistfully dreaming in lonely cathedral lights.

*   *   *

Yesterday's pages gave me a thousand chuckles as I noted how Moody "went vestigial," and became a confirmed Old Timer.

There were, of course, two strong-minded women whose love for the Old Paths profoundly moved him (Mrs. Cook and Mrs. Snow). And he had a strange bent for loving what they loved.

And Spurgeon had a backward influence upon him. When they were both young men, Spurgeon was two years Moody's senior. Moody was completely enamored of him. The first time he went to London (1867), he rushed post-haste to Metropolitan Tabernacle, shouldered his way in without a ticket, and sat in the high gallery, weeping throughout the service, "his eyes just feasting on Mr. Spurgeon."

This was unfortunate for a man in his formative period, because Spurgeon was the Greatest Throwback since Calvin. He went out of his way to point out each atavus from whom he derived his pedigree: "You can take a step from Paul to Augustine, and from Augustine to Calvin, and there you will pause with your foot in the air a long time before you find any such another. Luther dug his mental ore from Calvin's mine. And the Puritans got their wing and fire and force from the sage of Geneva."

Spurgeon began as a boy and, throughout his life, continued to ransack old London bookstores for Puritan volumes, which, fleeing from a superficial age, had lodged there for refuge. Hunted about, bound in sheepskins and goat skins; of whom he thought the current world was not worthy! He gave nine thousand of these folio fugitives a haven in his Westwood library; and gave *himself* a permanent cast from reading them. In analyzing his mental life, he boldly said, "I feel the shadow of their broad brims over *my* spirit!"

Because nearly all the Puritans wore beards, Spurgeon also grew one. And Moody grew one too, because he liked the way a beard looked on Spurgeon.

You may count upon it, when one man admires another so much that he copies his Van Dyke, he has already given himself to more serious imitations. Without Moody's being aware of it, his formative mind was stretched upon the same last as that which shaped John Owen and Richard Baxter—"I read everything Spurgeon ever writes!" Thus the sails of Moody's sermonic clipper were rigged ataunto, from the outset, with the Ancient Doctrines of Grace.

*   *   *

Still other forces moved into collusion to draw Moody back to the Old Paths. There was a race of ministers called "Bible preachers," who put an amazing emphasis upon the supremacy of the Word, and "refused to call a thing a sermon unless it rooted into and grew out of a text." They were swift to pierce with ridicule any discourse that was merely a bundle of "human observations, upon which, as a final gesture to inspire confidence, a text had been pasted."

Henry Moorhouse was an atavist of that sort. (See Chapter V) Born in 1840, he was a puny Lancashire lad, hell-bent-on-high by the time he was twenty. Wondrously saved just as he was about to commit suicide, he took to preaching at once; but being very poor missed the Professor's Booth; and, his personal appearance being weak, no one gave him books to read *about the Bible*. So he was off to a crippling start by having to go to it with nothing but a King James' Version. He became "a preacher whose sermons were only a string of proof texts." That being the case, it was annoying beyond all explanation, how thousands of *thinking* people, who should have known better, flocked after Moorhouse.

Moody and Moorhouse met in Dublin in the summer of 1867, Moody "speaking" in a little mission room. Within five minutes young Moorhouse "saw through Moody," that he was just a topic-talker, and told him after service with rasping Lancashire candor:

"Moody, you're on the wrong tack. If you will preach *God's words*, instead of *your words*, He'll make you a great power."

And did that raise a temperature in D. L.! He really thought he was good. Moorhouse planned to return to America with D. L., but the latter "gave him the slip." Moorhouse came to America on the *next* boat, followed to Chicago. Then was instrumental in giving Moody's sermonic nature a dreadful overhauling by demonstrating how people react toward Old Path Expositors. That is the provoking thing about these old time preachers — the people hear them gladly. Hallelujah Power overran Moody's church in a big red tide. And Moody said later, "I just couldn't keep back the tears. *I made up my mind I'd be a Bible preacher.*"

*   *   *

Spoken like a man, Dear Commoner!

But that is the hardest thing any dominie ever assays to do!

For Moody, it meant rising at 4 A. M. *the rest of his life!* (Torrey confirmed this.) "If I am going to get in any Bible study, I have to get up before the rest of the folks get up."

It meant, *locking up the commentaries until the Bible had finished with him!* I pore over the pages, not through the specs of some learned commentator, but with my own eyes."

It meant living with *one theme* until his soul began to move with the beat of the Holy Spirit. "I do not know how many hours I spent in studying out the Bible, one theme or another, until it just flowed out my finger tips."

It meant a steadfast practice of refraining from trying to tell people what he *thought* a certain passage *meant*, until first he had perfected himself in *quoting* exactly what it said. "What does it *say?* Never mind what you think it *teaches!*"

It meant "so thinking Scripture" that he could tell about ploughing a field or priming a pump in

Bible language. A thousand times he demanded of his students, "Tell us your experience in *Bible* language."

And it meant—*he stuck to one version until he mastered it*. He was interested that a certain new version was sent to Chicago as an expensive telegram. But he never used it himself. Stuck to the old King James'. I glance up at my shelves in Cedar-Palms and there is every version I ever heard about! But the only thing they have ever done for me is to bring a mental confusion that makes Babylon's polyglot plague seem relatively simple. Now I'm back for keeps on the Old King James'. . . .

With Moody, the achievement of "a Bibline disposition" (apologies to Stephen Charnock) meant more than anything else, a constant cry to the Spirit of Grace. Psalm 56:4—*"In God* I will praise His word"—is unintelligible, unless it means that our strongest hope for perennial enthusiasm toward the Book is a constant outpouring of Enabling Power. Someone once asked Moody, "How can I learn to use the Bible that way?" He replied,

"Arouse yourself to it! *And,* keep pleading with God! He'll assuredly help you!"

*   *   *

Thus it came to pass that by Thursday evening, June 22, 1873, which may be called the precise night the world awakening began, his "revision was complete." Not a single cracker dot upon him indicating the craft of a Dominie Machine! Just an "Old Timer" who, by a queer knight move, had bobbed up on the church checker board from a past era. A magnificent atavist!

What a strange race these old Bereans are! When they talk, one's interest is not slowed down by quotations from current philosophy. No, a thousand times, No! These atavists haven't spoken five minutes until one's soul hears the ravishingly sweet voice of Another; and one's eyes, though bathed in tears, begin to focus properly on the Face of Loveliness Divine.

I've laughed and wept too much over this humble man of Northfield! I suddenly find that, in conducting a clinic to study him, I've contracted his malady—Bible Atavism! The worst part of it is, having once contracted it, one never cares to get well. He stands in the ways, and *sees!* Begs for the Old Paths! Fears ever again to leave them, having found therein, for the first time, rest for his soul!

XII.

THE MARK HOPKINS OF THE RAGGED SCHOOL

John Pounds

"He might often have been seen on Saturday nights going round to the bakeshops to buy bread for his poor children to eat on Sundays, gathering it into his huge leathern apron and, when his money was all spent, standing still with a troubled look, searching in all his pockets for a few more coppers in order to secure yet one more loaf to add to his store." (*Letter from Rev. R. Timmins to William Edward Winks*)

THE MARK HOPKINS OF THE RAGGED SCHOOL

John Pounds

SOME of us whose nights are given to reading the book of records of the Chronicles (Esther 6:1, 2) find therein the narratives of ancient Mordecais, whose good works also are forgotten. Thereupon we inquire of our Latest Editions, "What honor and dignity hath been done to these men?" They reply: "Nothing; our publishers are gentlemen very sensitive to public tastes. They go in for volumes about such men as Saint Highly Publicized, even though the hacks of Scribblers' Lane have worn them thread-bare." "Surely, has no one honored Saint Almost Forgotten?" "But no! his box office value doth not warrant it."

Our deepest interest, however, is accorded the Sons of Cornelius whose biographies are written in one sentence:

"There was a certain man in Caesarea called Cornelius, a centurion of the band called the Italian and, a devout man, and one that feared God with all his house, who gave much alms to the people, and prayed always."

That's all! That's the entire Life.

For our part, we admit an Ahasuerus complex. We are determined that the King's apparel, and the King's horse, and the King's crown royal shall be set upon the heads of forgotten heroes of the Faith. Therefore, this last vignette in *Beacon Lights of Grace* is to the honor of John Pounds, the Mark Hopkins of the Ragged School. We wish to bring him through these printed pages on horseback!

*   *   *

We have always held the Seventh Earl of Shaftsbury in high esteem; particularly so since we read Hodder's *Life and Labors of the Seventh Earl of Shaftsbury*. But we were never more proud of Sir Anthony Ashley Cooper than when he stood, every inch the orator, at the opening of John Pounds Coffee Tavern in Plymouth and cried:

"I am a disciple of John Pounds!"

*   *   *

There is a marble tablet let into the outside walls of Plymouth's High Street Chapel, bearing luminous words:

Erected by Friends
As a Memorial of their esteem and respect
for
JOHN POUNDS
Who, while earning his livelihood
By mending shoes, gratuitously educated
And, in part, clothed and fed
Some hundreds of Poor Children.
He died suddenly
On the first of January, 1839
Aged 72 years
"Thou shalt be blessed: For they cannot
Recompense thee."

*   *   *

We just promised to bring John Pounds through these pages on horseback. But you must have noted, as he mounted, how the sinew of the hollow of his thigh was shriveled, and that he limped painfully. Naturally, since John Pounds is our hero, we do not desire him to have wrinkle, or spot, or blemish, or any such thing. Nevertheless, John Pounds *must* limp, for that is what made him John Pounds. . . .

When he was twelve years old, he fell into a dry dock and broke his right thigh-bone. Likely the fracture was neglected, and poor Pounds went lame and in pain, with the record on his face, for the next sixty years. This Bethel, however, conferred upon him seeing eyes and made his soul a watered garden. That dark day John became Israel: a devoted man on the quest for broken children. And after sixty years of it, an angel touched him and said:

"Come now to the heritage prepared for you!
Thou shalt be blessed; for these could not
recompense thee."

*   *   *

There is an entry, in the ancient chronicles, written by a Welshman, William Edward Winks, titled *Illustrious Shoemakers.* . . . When William Haryett, Minister of the Old School, and close friend of Spurgeon, came to the end, he passed his copy of *Illustrious Shoemakers* on to me. This is a good place to suggest, should some ancient saint decide to give you his books, receive them with gratitude. You are certain to find therein Fire-Books of a kind that are mournfully scarce today. Most likely you could not secure another copy of *Illustrious Shoemakers.* But the blessings of Mr. Winks' labors are partially yours; for *Beacon Lights of Grace* is much indebted to him.

Illustrious Shoemakers deals with such a company of great artists, poets, military men, ministers and business men, who began as shoemakers, that I have come to wonder if being a shoemaker isn't a prerequisite of honor. Was not my Henry Parsons Crowell a shoe clerk? and his father before him a shoe manufacturer? Was not D. L. Moody a shoe-drummer? my Christmas Evans the son of a shoe maker? my beloved Carey "a cobbler by the grace of God?" . . . So in this vignette we once again enter a room where a man sits and labors over a lap-stone. These are indeed still waters for thy servant; for John Pounds was a shoemaker!

* * *

Tom Pounds was a sawyer in a Portsmouth dock yard—and a good man at that. Day by day, he and his saw-man, armed with a long rip-saw, cut slabs from robust logs. These became planking for the hulls of British merchantmen. Tom's home was gladdened June 17, 1766, by the birth of a son, John. . . . John greatly admired his father, and was not at all vexed when his father bound him, at the age of twelve, as a shipwright apprentice in the same yard where his father, Tom, worked! Twelve, to be sure, is too tender an age to be bound out; and it took Shaftsbury to awaken the stupid British ship builders.

"Nimble" was the word used by the dock men when they spoke of John Pounds. "He was all over the place, like a wind-blown shadow: up the scaffolding and down again . . . and such a good lad. . . ." But a day came, a short time after he began, that John's foot slipped and he fell from a lofty scaffold into the dry dock.

For two years he suffered, unable to work, and when he was able to get around again, what could one with such an awful limp do? . . . He was glad to find an old man in High Street, Portsmouth, who offered him a cobbler's stool in the shoe shop. His limp would not bother him so much there. At fifteen, John completed his apprenticeship and became a journeyman shoemaker. . . . But he was never good at it. He seemed always to be grieving over something. . . .

* * *

In 1804, when John was thirty-eight, he ventured to become a tenant on his own account of a small weather-boarded tenement in St. Mary's Street. In the City Beside the Golden Gate you may see old cable cars, de-wheeled and put into back yards for play houses. And these old cables are just about the size, shape, length and breadth of Pound's combination home and cobbler's shop. There he lived and labored for the next thirty-five years. He came to love it: loved it so much that, when the angels came to get him, he out-did Lot's wife in looking back: "Was it not the dearest spot in the world?" And the reason for this affection you are now to be told.

* * *

John had a brother—a sea faring man—whose family was very large; all of the children fine-bodied Pounds, save one poor little twisted Tiny Tim. John's brother stood in need of assistance. John thought it over: he was a bachelor, lived in his snug "little" house (you may say that again!) ; he had plenty; he ought to help. Therefore he said to Brother Alfred, "If you wish, I could take a child in with me." Alfred said, "Which?" And John, who walked with a limp, said, "Tim."

Tim's poor little feet turned inward as he walked; he had to lift one over the other. Pounds made a "corrector" out of shoe soles, copying an expensive metal brace he once saw. . . . In a short time the boy was cured. Folks said, "What's got into John Pounds? He used always to be grieving over something. Now, he's the happiest man in Portsmouth!"

*   *   *

The nephew became old enough to set about learning his letters. John loved him so much that he resolved to do the work of a schoolmaster himself; and if he was to teach little Alfred, he ought to take another boy: "Children learn better if there are two of them." Whom should it be?

Right down St. Mary's Street a bay window overhung the sidewalk. And under that bay window a poor woman lived with her family in a space open to the street, open to frost and snow. One of her children was so marginal, that he was called "The Urchin."

There now! That was just the boy for whom Pounds was looking! So The Urchin came into the box car room to live. And may we say, another of the angels, who require no space, but do a lot of good, moved in, too. We really suspect that angel of drumming up shoe business—angels are such queer folks!

It was certainly unmistakable the way John's business grew.

Along with his "family and prosperity," John had a great idea: There were a lot of children in Portsmouth whose education and training were entirely neglected by their parents; children who ran about the streets ragged and destitute. . . . Why not pick up two, maybe three more? So there were two or three more, and of course two or three more angels. And bless me, those angels also turned out shoe drummers!

Even an angel, however, can get only a limited number of boys into a slim box car. Very well, then, even if more children couldn't *live* with John, he could have them around . . . *teach* them . . . get them books to read . . . cookies to eat . . . and clothing to wear.

He could, moreover, take them to Church on Sundays. So he crowded his pastor's church every Sunday with a swarm of boys. . . . Ah, my friends, that dear preacher was always sure of a good congregation! and he was sure of a good annual report under the head "Accessions!" "Pounds led practically all of his boys to Jesus."

Think of that for an evangelical funnel! A workshop and school combined, crowded for more than a quarter of a century with rag-a-muffins who were first saved, then clothed, put into their right minds;

and, finally, drawn off into the Kingdom! Do you blame me, reader, for calling John Pounds "the eighteenth century edition of Mark Hopkins"?

*   *   *

Of course these children grew up. Of course! And they became useful citizens: some of them powerful merchants, naval officers, and the like. . . . It was no unusual thing to see a great man in brass buttons walk down St. Mary's Street, enter the shoeshop, and immediately you would hear Saints' Laughter. And it was no uncommon thing, after John died, to see men of affairs resort to a little monument in the Portsmouth Cemetery . . . shamelessly weep awhile: quietly brush the tears away, and depart.

*   *   *

On Christmas Day, 1838, John, now seventy-two, was invited to take tea with "his friend, Mr. Edward Carter, Esquire." Mr. Carter had a surprise for John, but John didn't know it. After trifles and tea, Mr. Carter led John into his great drawing room. There on the wall was a magnificent oil painting, executed by the famous British artist, Shief.

And the subject of the wall-wide oil was *John Pounds!* John Pounds in the narrow room, with his last in his lap, surrounded by his boys! John looked thoughtfully for a moment, then shouted with delight: "Look! look! Tabby's in the picture, too," Sure enough, there was Tabby the Cat, looking up into John's face. . . . That's all John saw worthy of delight; Tabby looking up at him. . . . And if you ask me, I'm sure Tabby was purring.

*　　*　　*

Well, John, we've had you through the streets on the King's horse. We're sure you're not particularly proud of it now: you're hearing so much sweeter praise. And we doubt if you would have been particularly proud of it then—unless Tabby trotted 'long side.

But *we* are proud to have held your horse's halter as you rode! We have that much Ahaseurus in us.

*　　*　　*

We read somewhere, "All service ranks the same with God." Sure, John, the artist *should* have made a good painting! He had such a good subject in you!

*　　*　　*

The book is done . . . But we must add a matter which we first discovered in that Hoosier Library, in the dear days agone. It was something about the Borrowed glow; the Fire which maketh men God's Beacon Lights; and how men should conduct themselves when that glow rests upon them:

> "MOSES WIST NOT THAT THE
> SKIN OF HIS FACE SHONE
> WHILE HE TALKED
> WITH GOD."

INDEX

167